FANTASTIC BEASTS
AND WHERE TO FIND THEM™

THE ART OF THE FILM

DERMOT POWER

FOREWORD BY STUART CRAIG

HARPER DESIGN
An Imprint of HarperCollinsPublishers

ACKNOWLEDGEMENTS

I would like to thank Dan Moody for his unwavering dedication to
hunting down the art and artists that were scattered all over the globe.

Also Brandon at Framestore, for his endless patience with
my requests for comments and art, Niki Judd at Warner Bros. for
connecting all the dots, and Chris Smith, Terence Caven & Georgie
Cauthery at HarperCollins for giving me the space to do a book I
could be proud of.

Huge appreciation and admiration to J.K. Rowling, David Yates
and David Heyman for allowing me to be part of this fantastic journey,
and last but not least, Stuart Craig, who continues to be an inspiration
and mentor for all the artists lucky enough to spend time in his art
department.

Published in 2016 by
Harper Design
An Imprint of HarperCollins*Publishers*
195 Broadway
New York, New York 10007
Tel: (212) 207-7000
Fax: (855) 746-6023
harperdesign@harpercollins.com
www.hc.com

Distributed throughout North America by
HarperCollins Publishers
195 Broadway
New York, New York 10007

ISBN 978-0-06-257133-5

Printed and bound in USA

First Printing, 2016

◄◄ **NEWT'S CASE** In exploring how Newt enters his case, one idea we considered was to
have a shadow that magically cuts a stairway in to the ground – way too complicated
but it made a nice, iconic image. **DP**

CONTENTS

FOREWORD   7

INTRODUCTION   9

1   NEW YORK   12

2   MACUSA   54

3   NEWT'S CASE   82

4   THE FANTASTIC BEASTS   98

5   THE BLIND PIG   212

6   THE OBSCURUS   238

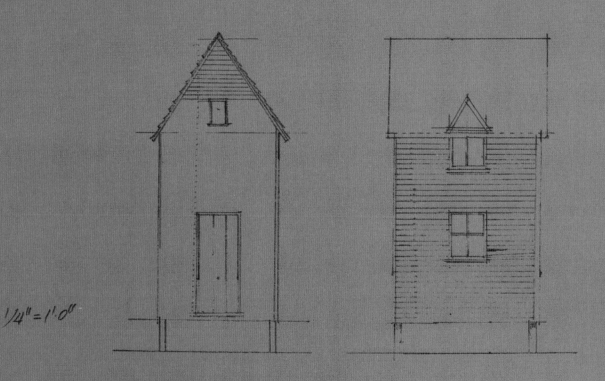

1/4" = 1'-0"

FOREWORD

All the illustrations in this book are computer generated.

Responsible for all these were seven concept artists, one man bands, working in-house. Also several more, often working in teams, in the Visual Effects Houses. Each was tasked, according to their specialities, with creating concepts or illustrations for manufactured props, physical sets, set extensions, creatures, creature habitats.

To sell an idea, 2D sketches are often used, but with creatures it can be as quick to build a 3D model, the start of a continuing process of building, rendering, compositing in which the model evolves into a highly detailed creature. A very technical exercise but the most important decisions taken during this process are not technical but artistic ones, concerning proportion, shape, character and mood.

Fast-developing software can mean huge programmes to learn and keep up with. But whether sketch or model and no matter how technically complicated, it is a work of art. A flick of the "brush" can be hugely significant.

It's pencil and paper, light and form but these artists can draw like Raphael and model with light like Caravaggio. It's magic made to look simple and that's hard.

STUART CRAIG

NEWT'S SHED There was much discussion about how 'tailored' Newt's world should be. In keeping with the notion that his primary concern is keeping the beasts happy and safe, he does just enough and doesn't worry too much about clean lines and perfect edges. The unfinished border of the wood hill supports this idea. **DP**

THE ART OF THE FILM

INTRODUCTION

My first introduction to the wizarding world of Harry Potter was when my twelve-year-old son was reading the books – he *loved* them and would not look up from the page until the particular instalment was finished. I had also heard from friends, who were reading the books to their younger children, who admitted that they were 'actually quite good' and that they couldn't put them down after the kids had gone to sleep.

Eventually I read them myself and saw that, even though they were aware of and occasionally influenced by fantasy books that had gone before, J.K. Rowling's world was very particular – familiar and real and contemporary, even when they were full of magic and wonder and mystery. It is this placing of the extraordinary alongside the very ordinary that makes her invented world so interesting to design and it was the guiding design philosophy in the early Harry Potter films as well as in *Fantastic Beasts and Where to Find Them*.

Stuart Craig, our production designer and guiding light in the Potter art department during the early 2000s, often reminded us to keep our designs 'real' – the magic would be more extraordinary and believable when framed by a world that had weight and structure and history. Hogwarts is extraordinary but we believe the architecture even when it is as strange as Dumbledore's triple tower.

I took these lessons with me to other films and franchises and found myself often quoting Stuart and referring back to him and the world he had evolved for all eight Potter films. The lessons learned about design were universal and long lasting.

So I was delighted when Stuart called me a decade later to ask if I would return to the fold for the latest J.K. Rowling wizarding adventure directed by David Yates and produced by David Heyman. Both Davids shared Stuart's belief in grounding our designs in reality when teasing out the 'design

narrative'* of a character, creature or place. J.K. Rowling's wonderfully evocative writing made our task much easier, and David Yates was wholly supportive of the approach: he would often say 'it must be believable – it must be intuitively true'.

In 2005, I attended a lecture Stuart delivered in Berlin about how the world of design was becoming digital and that film art departments should prepare for and embrace the new technologies. In the ten years since that lecture, tools developed for post-production – such as 3D set design, digital sculpting, photographic compositing techniques

---

* The 'design narrative' is very hard to explain in a single sentence without sounding pretentious, but is very important. It is finding the story of a design. A simple example is a tree blown by the wind. What is the tree trying to do? It's trying to grab light from the sun. How does it do this? It grows towards the sun. What is holding it back? Gravity and the wind and the earth. Once you have these story elements then

and animation – became available to concept artists and the pre-production team. The art department I joined for *Fantastic Beasts* had space for the traditional and the new: the draughting tables and pencils still favoured by a generation of designers, whose depth of experience was irreplaceable, and the newer, tech-savvy, mostly younger artists who sat in front of computer screens. Stuart was comfortable with both because the rules for good design are always the same, whether pencil on paper or pixels on a screen.

In the intervening years, the number of films that needed concept artists had expanded enormously as the studios invested in more and more big-budget visual effects-heavy films. And there were *many* more concept artists – the typical art department's two or three became six or seven, but the costume department also had their team, as did props, and creatures; in fact, any department that saw the value in having a design idea presented with visuals from sketch to fully rendered illustration. The biggest supplier of concept art became the VFX (visual effects) department, which split and branched in to several different teams attached to the various VFX houses all over the world. The VFX artists were now integral to the pre-production design phase of any film. And on *Fantastic Beasts* we were all on site at Leavesden sharing and evolving the design together, guided by Stuart, the Davids* and J.K. Rowling herself.

We creatives who were lucky enough to have spent time guided by Stuart at Leavesden Studios, just outside but not too close to the distracting bustle of London, in our very own Hogwarts, were given the time and space to be the designers that J.K. Rowling's wizarding world needed and deserved.

---

* We did call David Yates and David Heyman 'the Davids'. 'Do you think it will get past the Davids?' was the most common question about a design.

This book is a small sample of all that wonderful creativity. Ten years ago we had hundreds of images to choose from; now I had thousands. And in selecting from them it was a fantastic opportunity for me to re-connect with all of the artists and gather their thoughts on what inspired them to create the images.

I have elected to present this gallery of their art in chapters, to allow you to experience each key element of the film within its own frame, as it were. And within each chapter I have included work that showcases the evolution of the creative process: from the earliest sketches and designs produced as we sought to find the best, most imaginative way of expressing J.K. Rowling's vision on screen, to more confident art created when we knew we were close to capturing the perfect beast design or location. It was a lengthy and exacting process – where some creatures would appear before us almost like magic but others would prove very hard to find – but the journey was always a fascinating and rewarding one.

We begin with New York City (p. 12), and the sights and wonders of its locations inhabited by New Yorkers both No-Maj and magical, and the extraordinary re-creation of the city during its rise in the 1920s. Everything from the dockside customs hall and bank to the splendour of Shaw Tower and grimy streets where ordinary folk like Jacob live in their tenement buildings. All this and more was created thanks to the talents of concept artists Peter Popken, Tom Wingrove and Hayley Easton-Street.

These same talents would help a wider team capture Stuart Craig's vision of MACUSA's wonderful headquarters hidden within the Woolworth Building (p. 54), where the dazzling open spaces of the upper floors sit above the altogether darker, subterranean levels. Newt's case – and the fantastic beasts housed inside it – would prove a very different location to help realize, and the two sections on pp. 82–211 showcase the work of many artists as they explored and finally nailed the look of the extraordinary

beasts that Newt is taking care of, and the environments in which they live.

We are then swept into the seedy underworld speakeasy of The Blind Pig, haunt of magical lowlife keen to avoid the attentions of Aurors, while the goblin house band fills the joint with jazz music (p. 212).

As we reach our climax, we come face to face with the Obscurus (p. 238), the dark force which is threatening to destroy the city unless Newt can find a way to stop it.

Finally, it needs to be acknowledged that the concept art is not the only 'art' produced by the art department and of course it is not the only design, just a part of it, like an iceberg peeking above the water. Beautiful plans and elevations, fantastic card models and miniatures, maquettes, graphics and of course the sets themselves, the scenic paintings, sign writing and monumental sculptures – but that's for another book.

This is about the images. Let them take you on a journey.

DERMOT POWER

LIST OF ARTISTS

AB	Adam Baines
ABR	Arnaud Brisebois
ABRO	Adam Brockbank
AV	Arnaud Valette
BK	Ben Kovar
DB	Dan Baker
DFO	David Frylund Otzen
DH	Daren Horley
DP	Dermot Power
DS	David Simpson
FC	Francesco Corvino
FV	Frédéric Valleur
GA	Giles Asbury
GM	Gurel Mehmet
HES	Hayley Easton-Street
JC	Jim Cornish
JJ	Jama Jurabaev
KS	Kresten Smedemark
KT	Kouji Tajima
MB	Michael Borhi
MK	Max Kostenko
MM	Martin Macrae
MS	Molly Sole
PC	Paul Catling
PG	Pablo Grillo
PP	Pietro Ponti
PPOP	Peter Popken
RB	Rob Bliss
RJ	Rob Jensen
SC	Samantha Combaluzier
SCR	Stuart Craig
SM	Stephen Molyneaux
SR	Sam Rowan
TR	Tania Richard
TW	Tom Wingrove
VH	Victor Hernandez

1

NEW YORK

HMS TEMERESI I built the front part of the *HMS Temeresi* in 3D to include the physical set we were building at the studio. I worked with the art director to enable Stuart Craig and supervising art director James Hambidge to show what you would see as Newt approached New York for the first time. **TW**

AERIAL SHOT OF NEW YORK This shot was to help establish where MACUSA would appear in the skyline. The art department went to great lengths to decipher from reference images which buildings existed at the time of the story. **TW**

NEW YORK SKYLINE The skyline of 1920s New York is strikingly modern, with buildings we still recognize today, whereas most ships of the period are either sunk or scrapped. Luckily enough, we were able to reconstruct a typical ocean liner from a model ship and antique drawings pulled from archives. **PPOP**

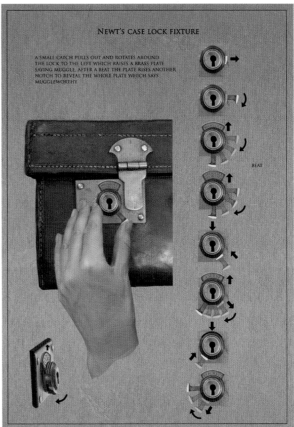

A SMALL CATCH PULLS OUT AND ROTATES AROUND
THE LOCK TO THE LEFT WHICH RAISES A BRASS PLATE
SAYING MUGGLE. AFTER A BEAT THE PLATE RISES ANOTHER
NOTCH TO REVEAL THE WHOLE PLATE WHICH SAYS
MUGGLEWORTHY.

BEAT

↑ **NEWT'S CASE LOCK FIXTURE / MS**

← **CUSTOMS HALL** This is my favourite illustration and
it shows how a warehouse in Bedford UK could be
transformed into a bustling New York dock with a 'little
help' courtesy of set dressing and green screen allowing
digital extensions. **PPOP**

NEW YORK STREET SCENE Stuart and senior art director Dave Alday laid out the plan for these looming structures as symbols of the establishment and obstacles to Jacob as he embarks on his journey. Partly built on the backlot of Leavesden Studios, they were later combined with digital backgrounds. Darker painted clouds in the sky foreshadow events to come... **PPOP**

THE BANK The lower half of the bank was to be a practical set with the upper half extended digitally. Using reference images of Tweed Courthouse in Manhattan I built a 3D model and then painted a concept to show how this should look. **HES**

EXTERIOR OF JACOB'S APARTMENT The first stage of a digital set extension design is to create a 3D model and set up a potential shot like this [inset]. The grey shows the physical set build and the green represents the VFX set extension; this gives a clear guide so everyone knows exactly what will be achieved 'in camera'.

The next stage of the process is to paint the 3D model and lock down the design of the VFX set extension [main image]. The street in which Jacob's apartment is located was based on the tenement streets of the Lower East Side in Manhattan, small shops, low cost apartments and run-down architecture – in stark contrast to the more prestigious city streets by Shaw Tower, the Bank and City Hall. **HES**

EXTERIOR OF JACOB'S APARTMENT After the scene outside Jacob's apartment had been shot I was given still frames from the rushes (*left & right*).

Using a combination of 3D model and 2D background I then painted over the green-screen area to show exactly what the VFX set extension should look like [main images]. The VFX team could then follow this design when they completed their work.

The architecture for the tenement buildings was based on Manhattan's Lower East Side: Orchard Street and the surrounding area. The elevated railway was based on a historic building at 238th Street, and the warehouse was taken from a street by Manhattan Bridge. I went to NYC with Stuart Craig to look at the architecture and photograph key buildings. Using a combination of the photographs I took and also historic reference I created the look of the extended street. **HES**

"THIS ILLUSTRATION WAS TO INVESTIGATE THE AMOUNT OF SERIOUS DAMAGE THAT A STAMPEDE OF ESCAPING CREATURES MIGHT CAUSE TO JACOB'S APARTMENT. AT THE SAME TIME, STUART WAS KEEN TO REFERENCE EVERYDAY LIFE IN THE TENEMENT BUILDINGS AND SURROUNDINGS AS DOCUMENTED IN CONTEMPORARY PHOTOGRAPHY."

INTERIOR OF JACOB'S APARTMENT / PPOP

DESIGN IDEA FOR SHAW TOWER This is an idea for the main entrance to the Shaw Tower. The spikes on the outer ring of the logo remained from an earlier version when 'Shaw' was then called 'Thorne'. **PPOP**

EARLY DESIGN OF SHAW TOWER This was when we were using the Radiator building (Bryant Park hotel) as inspiration. **TW**

SHAW TOWER This is the final design for the Shaw Tower. I worked with Stuart Craig to develop his vision. Stuart wanted to fine tune the design over time. I attempted to show the building in a gloomy atmospheric light. **TW**

SHAW TOWER INTERIOR A slick design for Shaw's office space situated in lower Manhattan high above Trinity Square. Art Deco was the latest fashion and represented the luxury and glamour of a millionaire's lifestyle. **PPOP**

SHAW SR.'S OFFICE We imagined Shaw Tower to be situated in lower Manhattan, so he could have that stunning view from his office to Trinity Place. **PPOP**

SHAW TOWER INTERIOR I assumed that the office of a millionaire like Shaw would contain furniture from all over the world. Further, he would celebrate the Art Deco style that represented modernity and progress in the early 1920s. Chinese designs, particularly from Shanghai, were very fashionable then and added a touch of exoticism to the interior. **PPOP**

VIEW FROM SHAW TOWER In this view Stuart wanted to make sure we saw through to Brooklyn Bridge but also keep the tall, impressive city buildings very visible. We look past digital extensions of the Department Store and City Hall sets, with the iconic Manhattan Municipal, Thurgood Courthouse, Emigrants Bank, Surrogates Court and Park Row architecture in the street beyond. **HES**

IDEA FOR THE NSPS CHURCH This was the very first concept I did working for Stuart. It was a great honour to be a part of the team and working for some of the most talented people in the industry. I worked under Stuart's guidance to establish an early idea of the NSPS church and its setting. **TW**

VIEW FROM SHAW TOWER This view was based on the architecture that would have been visible from Trinity Place in Manhattan: we see across the roof of Trinity Church to the buildings on Broadway. I built a 3D model of the area and then used a combination of photographs I had taken along with historic reference books to piece together the buildings that would have been visible in the 1920s. **HES**

GOLDSTEIN APARTMENT EXTERIOR This is the first pass of a painted 3D concept to show how a potential shot of the Goldstein apartment might look, and the architecture we would see in the streets beyond. The brownstone buildings were based on a residential street in Harlem with the iconic Met Life Tower and 1920s Madison Square Garden building (now demolished) in the background. **HES**

NEW YORK STREET SCENE Stuart had collected an extensive amount of research when scouting in NYC. Based on this we recreated our own New York street sets to best suit the story and production needs. Whilst Hayley was working on the 3D models, I was illustrating extended cityscapes. **PPOP**

NEW YORK STREET SCENE The opposite view of the above image. **PPOP**

↑ **NEW YORK STREET SCENE** This is one of many studies we did for the New York street sets. Since we were building all exterior sets in London we eventually got exactly what we needed to tell the story. The challenge was to combine the buildings in such a way that we'd achieve a variety of angles that suggest different locations. **PPOP**

↓ **CITY HALL EXTERIOR** Using the same process described on p. 44, but taking architecture from surrounding streets in Manhattan, I extended the street beyond City Hall. **HES**

CITY HALL EXTERIOR Using a combination of architecture from our location in Liverpool, and also Chambers Street in Manhattan, I created this concept to show what the final VFX set extension would look like for City Hall. The buildings of Chambers Street were chosen to complement the imposing architecture of City Hall. I used a combination of a basic 3D model that I built, along with my own photographs and historic images, to extend the street. **HES**

NEW YORK STREET SCENE I've never before done so much research for my illustrations as I've done for *Fantastic Beasts*. The attention to detail and accuracy of architecture was immense. I sometimes felt like I had to build a whole city from scratch and then populate it with people, shops, vehicles, signs, ads, and so on. An endless task in defiance of any deadline. **PPOP**

NEW YORK It was the attention to detail that turned our film set into a typical New York street scene. **PPOP**

↑ **NEW YORK STREET SCENE** This is a revamp of a set used earlier in the film and turned into a derelict building. Stuart noted that a skyscraper under construction seemed a nice metaphor for a rising metropolis of that period. **PPOP**

← **NEW YORK STREET VIEW** One of the processes that Stuart Craig brought with him from Harry Potter was that the design of each set would early on involve the construction of a cardboard model, to help everyone visualize the scale and geometry of the location and help the director plan his shots. This concept was adapted from one of those cardboard models, with the addition of lighting, composition, mood and narrative. **PPOP**

↑ **THE DERELICT SCHOOL** An establishing view of the school. **TW**

➡➡ **THE DERELICT SCHOOL** This was part of the sequence of Graves giving chase through the abandoned school. I worked for Stuart and the art director and built the set in 3D, conceptualizing the shot to show the destruction of Graves' enchantment as it tore through the wall. **TW**

↑ JACOB'S BAKERY WINDOW In amongst the standard loaves in the window, on a special display shelf are baked versions of the fantastic beasts that Jacob encountered. There is an Erumpent loaf, a paczki-style Niffler, a pretzel Occamy and an iced Demiguise like a Polish Babka. It was a fun challenge to find a cake style that would embody each creature. **MS**

← CONCEPT OF A STREET SCENE I like this concept because it covers all aspects of production design: a set build with architectural detail, prop design, costumes, graphics and digital set extension. **PPOP**

➔➔ THE MACUSA STAIRCASE This image was all about light, space and temperature. You can't see the vast vertical space above Newt as he climbs the stairs but you can suggest it with angled shadows. **ABRO**

2

MACUSA

❝WORKING TO STUART'S VISION, I PAINTED THIS SHOT TO DEPICT THE SCALE OF THE MACUSA BUILDING IN WHAT COULD BE ITS PERIOD SETTING. STUART REFERENCED MANY ICONIC IMAGES OF AERIAL VIEWS FROM SKYSCRAPERS THAT WERE UNDER CONSTRUCTION AS A GREAT WAY OF SEEING NEW YORK AS IT GREW IN THE 1920S.❞

MACUSA / TW

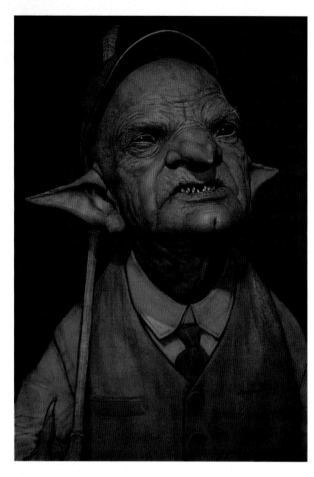

⬆ **RED THE DWARF** Alternative design for Red, MACUSA's dwarf lift operator, with his stick for poking at the elevator buttons. **RB**

⬆ **RED THE DWARF / RB**

⬆ **RED THE DWARF** Up-close design, made to look more gnarly and cantankerous. **RB**

➡ **LIFT OPERATION PANEL** This works by pressing the button of the room required using the staff and then setting it in motion by cranking the handle below to set the desired speed for travel. The button layout corresponds to the floor level layout of MACUSA and you can see from it that there are several absent floors in the building. **MS**

➡ **MACUSA INTERIOR** Here I attempted to illustrate the scale and height of the MACUSA interior, and the endless levels and floors. We played with the idea of five floors penetrating below the entrance level into the obscure and ominous recesses below. **TR**

⬆ MACUSA INTERIOR Tina is being questioned by the MACUSA High Council. This high-angle image uses light and atmosphere, and an enhanced emblem on the floor, to frame Tina, drawing the eye to her central position and conveying a sense of her isolation in front of the group. **TR**

➡ MACUSA INTERIOR This was my first task for Stuart. The setting of MACUSA was based on the Woolworth Building, a skyscraper in Lower Manhattan designed by Cass Gilbert. For the purpose of the film, the interior was gutted to create a cathedral-like space, illuminated by strong shafts of light similar to Bernice Abbot's photographs of Penn Station, removing any sense of an interior bound and constricted by conventional floors and ceilings. The striped marble adorning the walls was inspired by the Sienna Cathedral. Central to the illustration is an elaborate arched structure referencing the Albert Memorial and housing a group of bronzed sculptures, composed in the manner of Rodin's Burghers of Calais and paying tribute to the Salem Witch Trials. **TR**

THE PENTAGRAM OFFICE Set in the upper levels of the MACUSA building sits the Pentagram Office where the council debates important matters, and where Tina is questioned. Stuart referenced the interior of the House of Lords for the design of the chamber. We played with the deepness of the central floor, as well as the idea of having a railing around the perimeter to enhance Tina's isolation. In the end, we settled on darkening the floor and illuminating the emblem. **TR**

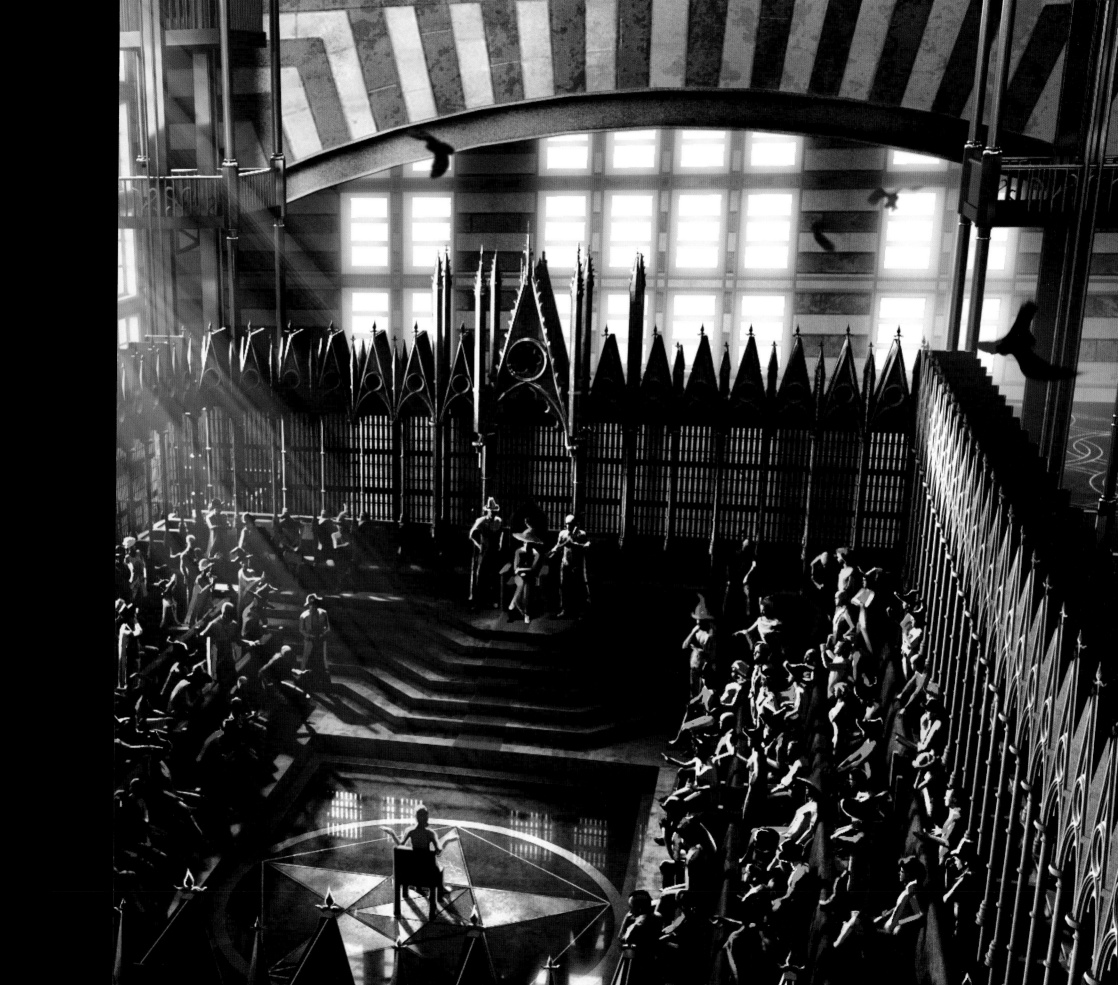

‘ A COLOUR AND MOOD
TWEAK TO THE MACUSA SET TO
ENSURE IT WAS IN KEEPING WITH
THE ESTABLISHED HARRY POTTER
WORLD AESTHETIC. ’

MACUSA INTERIOR / DP

↑ THE TYPING POOL This was my favourite task from Stuart. The Typing Pool sits in the depths of the MACUSA basement levels, occupied by self-operating typewriters spawning documents in the form of origami rats. Stuart composed an orthographic network of tubes and piping similar to London's famous Tube Map. I used Stuart's diagram as reference to weave and compose a 3D model of the environment in Maya. We then played with various camera lenses and angles to create a sense of endlessness similar to the fields of crosses in a war cemetery. **TR**

↑ **THE TYPING POOL** Working directly for Stuart to develop the Typing Pool set, this was one of two images I produced. I built the catacombs and pipes in 3D and produced many iterations showing the arrangements of the cascading pipes. **TW**

➡➡ **THE TYPING POOL** This is the reverse of the Typing Pool set showing Newt and Tina as he goes to collect his wand permit. I wanted to keep the tone dark and moody, dank and dusty, with an occasional scattering of origami rats as they go about their tasks. **TW**

↑ INTERROGATION CHAMBER I worked with the set art director to allow Stuart to figure out the mood and lighting of the interrogation cells in the depths of MACUSA. **TW**

← THE MACUSA CELLS This was a shot of the corridor leading up to the cells. Stuart was keen to develop the decayed patina of the cast iron. **TW**

DEATH CELL CHAIR / MS

→ **CONCEPT OF BLACK MOLLIES** This shows a school of black mollies shoaling to form Grindelwald's head as he speaks. Difficult to do in a still image, this probably needs an animatic to really show what's going on; however, the concept was dropped before I had the chance. **PC**

THE MACUSA CELLS This was the first of two images showing Newt's journey into the MACUSA cells. I built all the vaults in 3D, rendered and painted these shots. It was my attempt at capturing some of the mood and atmosphere that was so resonant in the Harry Potter films. **TW**

AN UNUSED DESIGN OF A SASQUATCH This is an incidental character spending a night in the cells at MACUSA. I included his house-elf buddy who, post-brawl, is unwilling to engage in any form of conversation. **RB**

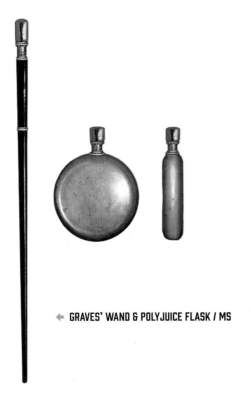

GRAVES' WAND & POLYJUICE FLASK / MS

DESIGN ITERATIONS FOR NEWT'S WAND (1–16) We ran through a lot of these, exploring materials and styles that would have an affinity with the character's passion for the natural world, travel, and adventure. Designs in bone were quickly thrown over in favour of those made from fossils, which felt more appropriate for Newt's conservationist character, being precious remnants of ancient creatures as opposed to possibly fashioned or hunted trophies. The script specified the stem be made of hornbeam and this along with the chosen belemnite handle makes the wand appear quite modest at first glance. When held up to the light, however, the material reveals itself as semi-transparent and partly opalescent in places. The texture of the ancient sea squid is discernible on the surface through the preservation of its tiny veins. I thought this would provide a link to the animal kingdom and also serves as a powerful asset for a Magizoologist's wand. **MS**

FINAL DESIGNS FOR THE AUROR, PERCIVAL GRAVES' WAND (17–21) Elegant, fashioned in a dark wood and finished in silver, it is the perfect complement to what would be the final costume design created for him by Colleen Atwood and her team. **MS**

VARIOUS ITERATIONS FOR QUEENIE'S WAND (22–28) I was exploring the shapes of shells and flowers and was given information that mother of pearl was commonly used by wand makers during this period. The shell shape created in this material seemed to resonate with the warmth and ultra feminine nature of the character. **MS**

FINAL DESIGNS FOR THE HERO CHARACTERS' WANDS (29–33) Laid out together, it was important to compare them in design and length and check that they felt right in relation to each other given the wide spectrum of characters using them. Looking left to right, Graves' wand is longer than the rest which speaks of his considerable power and drive. The simple single piece of turned wood used for Tina's is in keeping with her humble and earnest character. Likewise, Newt's wand reflects his connection with, but not his domination of, beasts, with its fossil handle. Queenie's wand is elegant and feminine but not showy, whereas the delicate silver art deco style detail latticed over the cut amethyst on Seraphina Picquery's wand befits the witch's overt prowess. **MS**

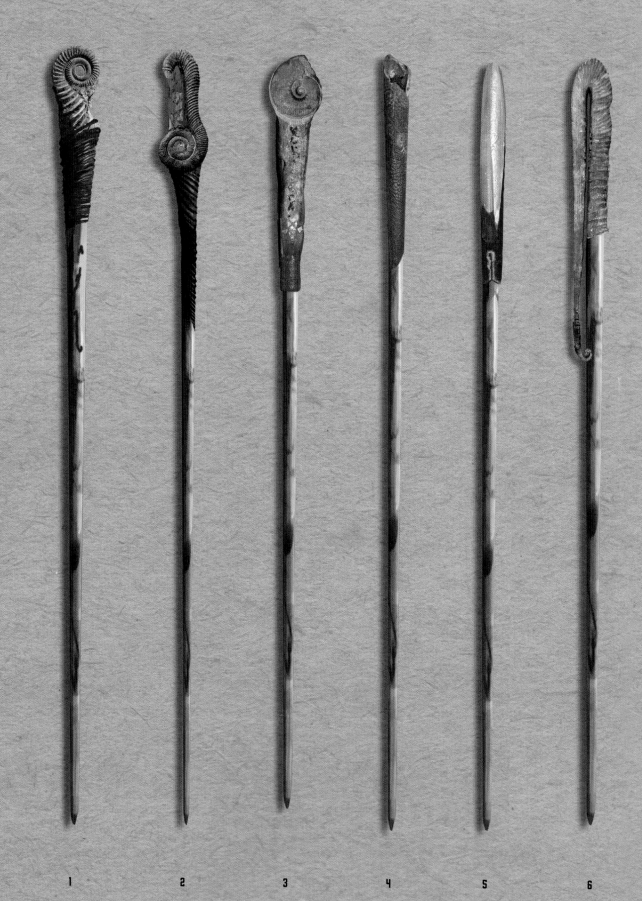

1   2   3   4   5   6

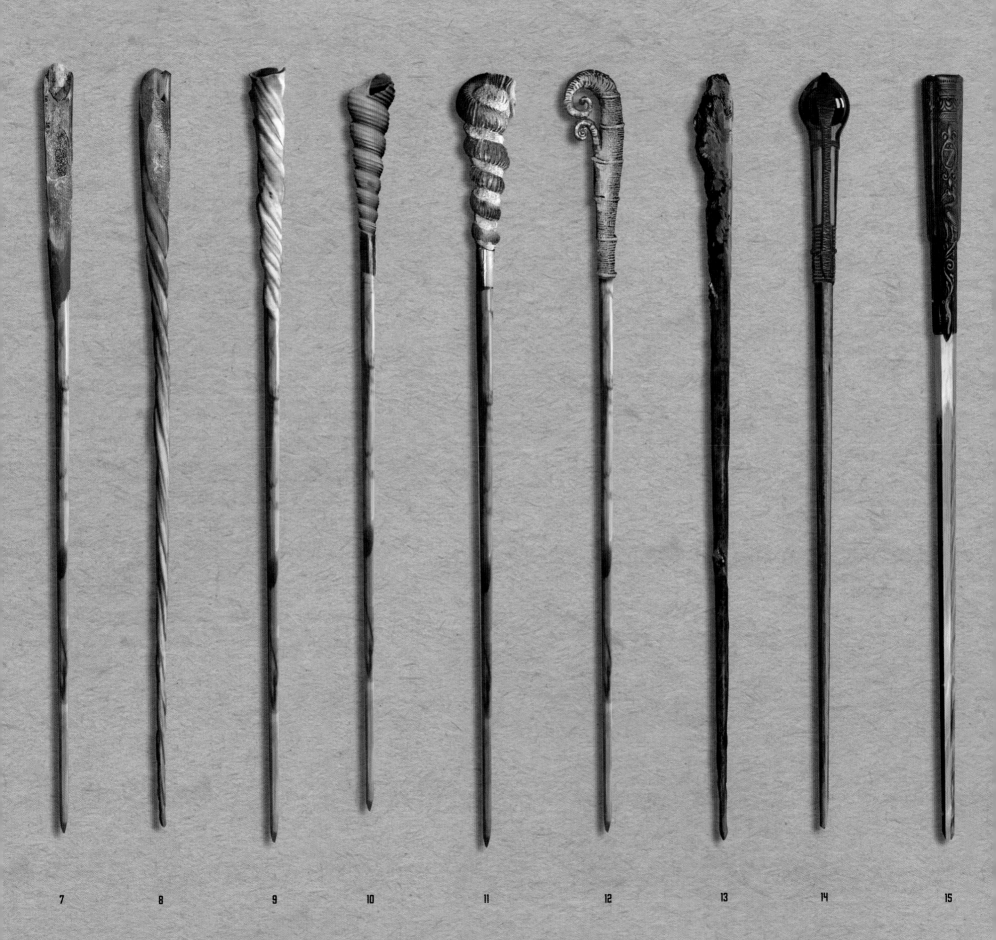

7   8   9   10   11   12   13   14   15

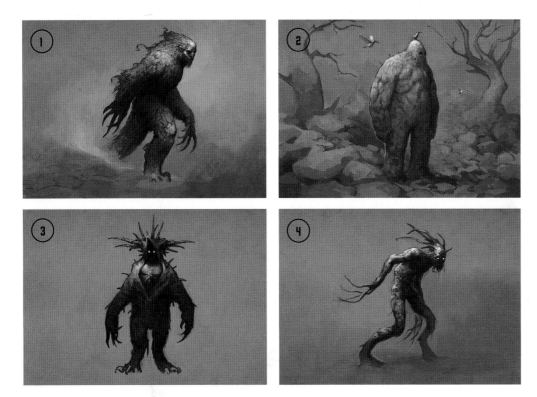

SASQUATCH DESIGNS With this design I wanted something that looked like it existed in a very harsh and physically demanding environment (1). I liked the idea of an environment of moss covered stones, here the Sasquatch is so still it seems like part of the landscape (2). The Sasquatch has its origin in Native American folk tales. Here a shaman wears an enchanted bearskin to become the creature, but it is not clear who is possessing who (3). Most of my other designs for the Sasquatch were for huge, powerful creatures. I liked the idea of doing something thinner and more tentative (4). **BK**

SASQUATCH I really enjoyed drawing this image of a Sasquatch in jail. **PC**

SASQUATCH I just thought about my morning commute to work by train and all the armpits I've encountered. **BK**

➡➡ **THE MACUSA CELLS** This was the second of two images showing Newt's journey into the MACUSA cells. **TW**

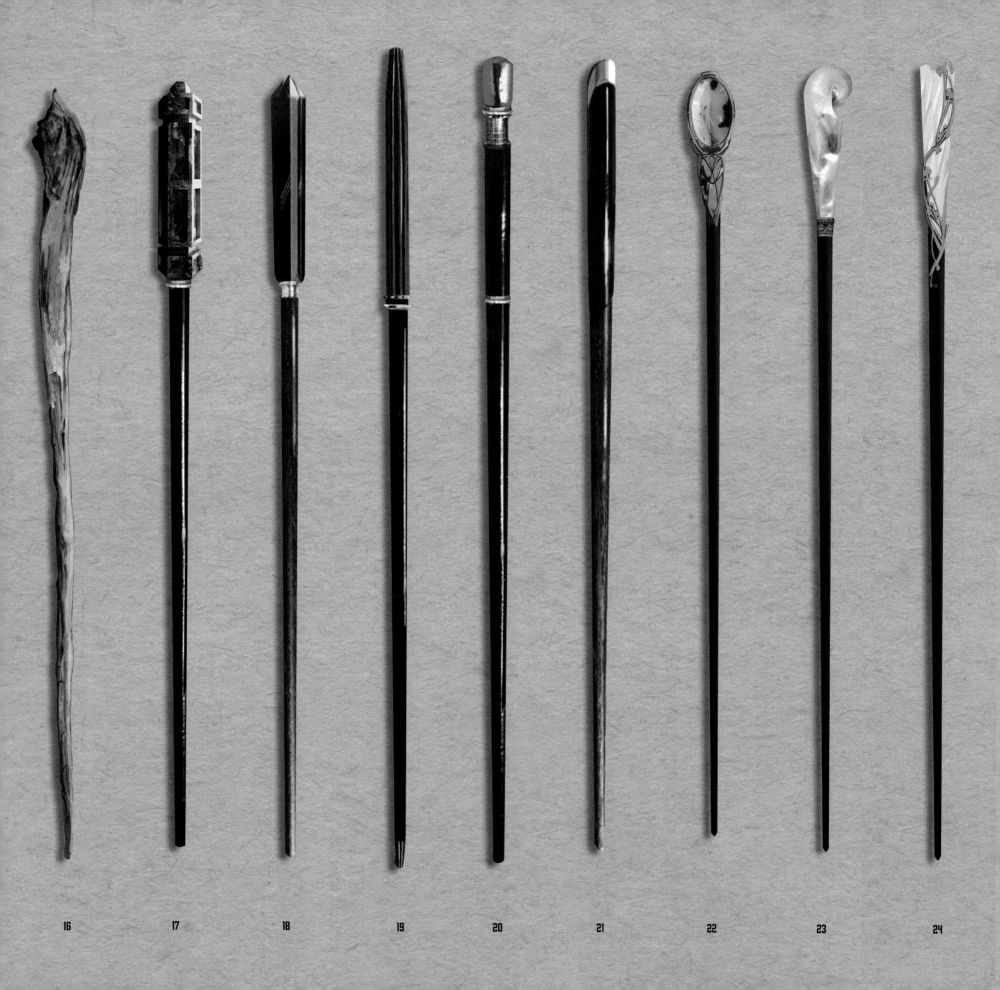

16   17   18   19   20   21   22   23   24

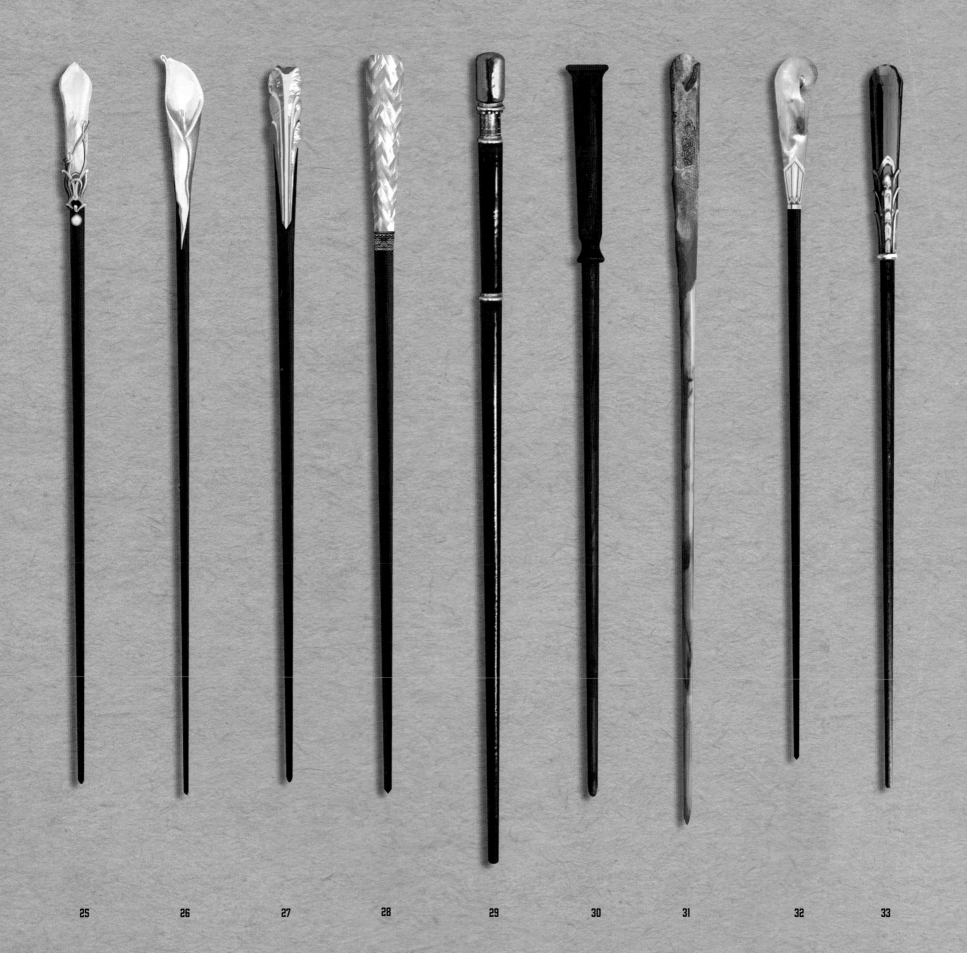

25   26   27   28   29   30   31   32   33

‘THIS SCENE SHOWS NEWT AS HE IS BEING PUT INTO THE CELLS IN THE DEPTHS OF MACUSA. IT WAS MY ATTEMPT AT REFERENCING SOME OF THE TONE AND MOOD CREATED BY DERMOT POWER, ADAM BROCKBANK & ANDREW WILLIAMSON IN THE ORIGINAL HARRY POTTER CONCEPT ART.’

THE MACUSA CELLS / TW

3
NEWT'S CASE

NEWT'S CASE Ominous dark shadows with light from the case suggesting a portal to a world below. **DP**

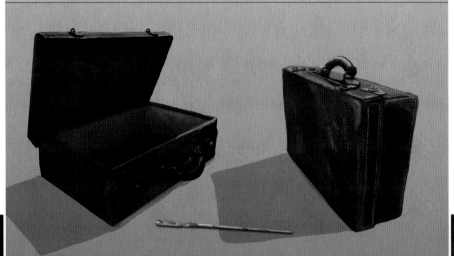

NEWT'S CASE Early prop design of the case and wand. **MS**

NEWT'S CASE How do you make something as everyday as a case have more presence in a scene? Long dark shadows. It's probably hard to find a spot in New York where the evening sun would make it past the tall buildings. Maybe there were more gaps in the 1920s city. **DP**

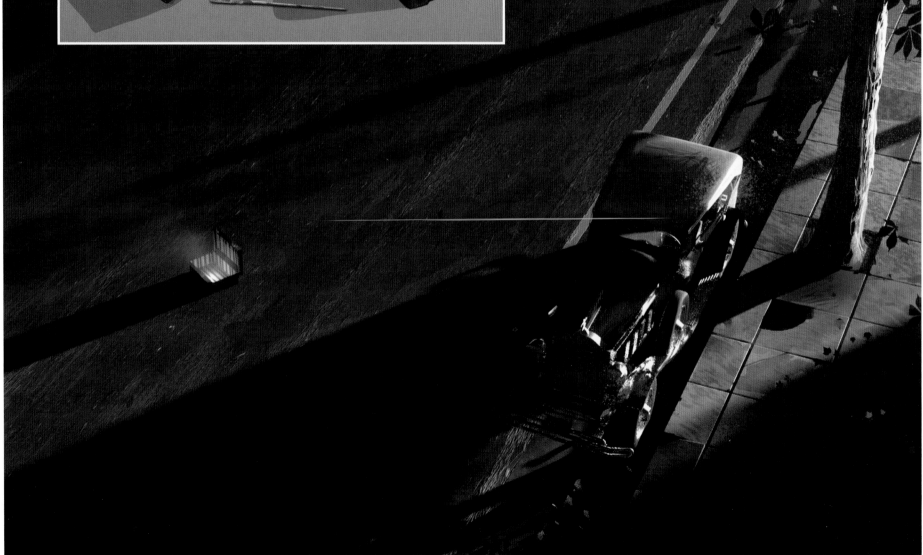

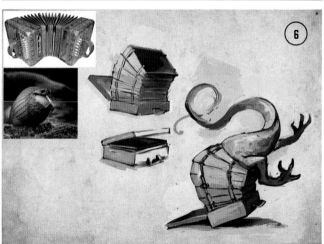

1 We explored a lot of ideas as to how Newt could enter the world inside his case. I liked the idea that this would be a mechanical rather than magical process.

2 The case needed a way of preventing its contents from escaping. This idea was based on a simple mantrap but in the end it was a bit too like something from Terry Pratchett's Discworld and that would have been sacrilegious.

3 Here an old fashioned elevator provides access to the hidden world of the case. I liked the idea that this magical door would be something clattering and mechanical.

4 Here the case propels itself using magical clockwork. I liked the contrast between this and the more ethereal magic of wands and spells.

5 How would Newt capture large creatures with his case? The idea here was that it would be like a bullfight – only one where the bull disappears into the fighter's cape. I liked the idea that this would mimic the street magician's most basic disappearing trick rather than a display of real magic.

6 This case can trap creatures larger than itself, but like a snake it takes a while to swallow them. **BK**

↑ **IDEA FOR AN ALTERNATIVE TO THE SHED** Here, inspired by the Pitt River Museum, Newt's world is crammed full of artefacts he has picked up on his travels. **DP**

← **IDEA FOR AN ENTRANCE TO NEWT'S SHED** How to get in and out of the shed? This was an early concept making use of the already established idea that paintings in the wizarding world are 'alive'. The Niffler escapes through a painting of a staircase inspired by Charles Wilson Peale's 'staircase group'. **DP**

→ SHED INTERIOR Newt's shed is this film's version of Hagrid's hut – one of my favourite sets from the Harry Potter movies. It was great to work on a similar Stuart Craig design for *Fantastic Beasts and Where to Find Them*. The shed is full of the stuff Newt has picked up on his travels to care for the beasts. **DP**

⬆ **A LOCATOR** I based this design for the Locator on the brass that I used to polish at home for pocket money when I was about eleven. **RB**

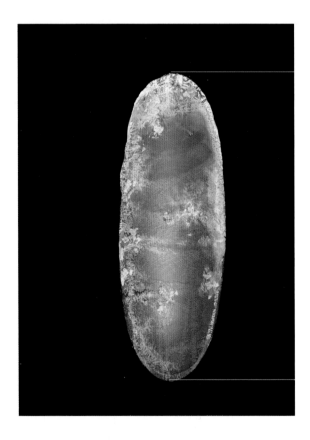

⬅ **ASHWINDER EGG** The properties of an Ashwinder egg are very specific: laid by the Ashwinder snake the egg is hot to the touch and capable of combusting to create a fire in flammable surroundings. It was scripted as having been frozen by means of a spell, making it a tradable ingredient for love potions. We tried to find a finish that would convey this magical oxymoron. I referenced ice textures, and the final frozen shell was made irregular so it would retain some of the natural look of a soft snake egg. **MS**

⬆ **BILLYWIG EGGS / MS**

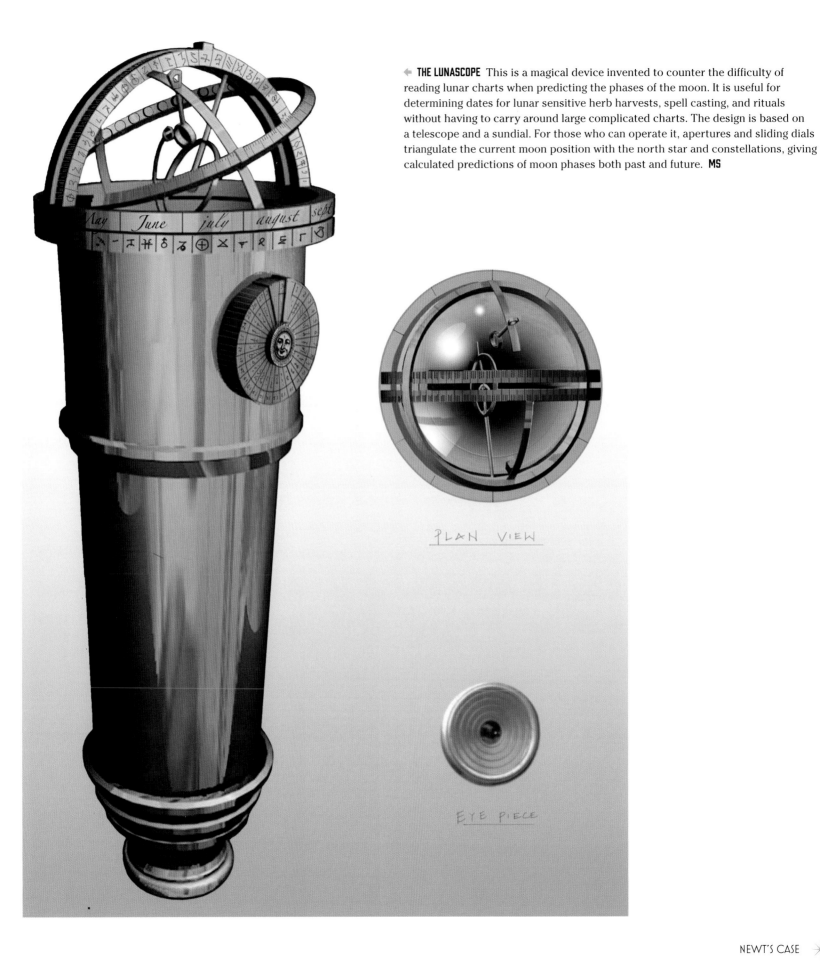

THE LUNASCOPE This is a magical device invented to counter the difficulty of reading lunar charts when predicting the phases of the moon. It is useful for determining dates for lunar sensitive herb harvests, spell casting, and rituals without having to carry around large complicated charts. The design is based on a telescope and a sundial. For those who can operate it, apertures and sliding dials triangulate the current moon position with the north star and constellations, giving calculated predictions of moon phases both past and future. **MS**

PLAN VIEW

EYE PIECE

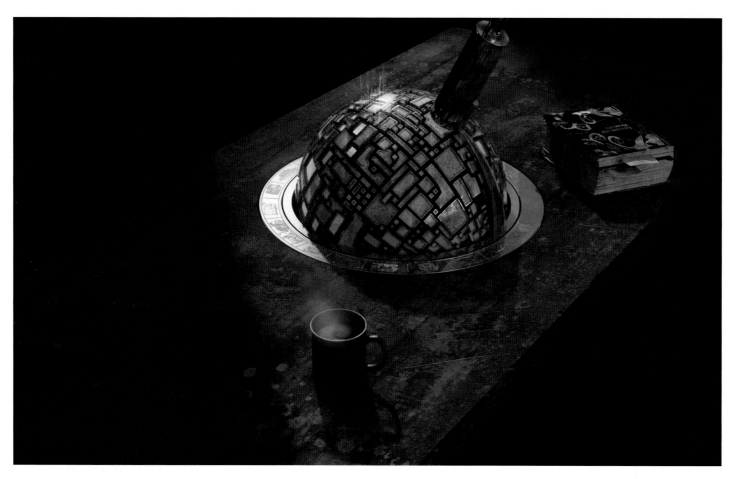

➡ **NEWT'S SHED** This was developed from a classic Stuart Craig design: something familiar but with a twist! The design itself was inspired by the weatherbeaten seaside huts you might see in the dunes along the English coast. Stuart insisted that the 'feet' be a little too thin for the structure, which gives it a light, nimble feel. **DP**

⬆ **ABANDONED IDEA FOR A 'NAVIGATOR' FOR NEWT'S SHED** Each environment is represented by a cell on the globe that Newt can examine with his telescope. Eventually this was deèmed way too complicated. **DP**

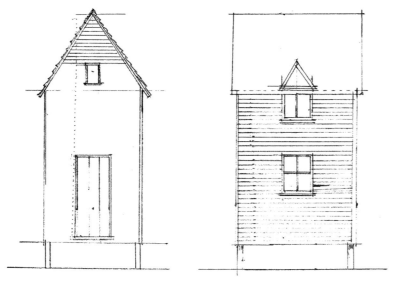

1/4" = 1'.0"

⬅ **SKETCH OF NEWT'S SHED / SCR**

➡ **NEWT'S SHED** We explored the idea that there was no central location for the shed. When Newt selected a creature's home world (using the navigator or maybe a magical map) then the environment outside the shed became that world. It was important that the shed was embedded in the environment as if it has always been there, meaning it didn't travel. **DP**

➡➡ **NEWT'S SHED** A frame from an animation that I created to demonstrate how the shed would exist in whatever creature environment Newt wanted to visit. The icicles and snow build up, reinforcing the idea that the shed did not 'travel' there. **DP**

6 AS THE DESIGN OF NEWT'S WORLD
EVOLVED IT BECAME SMALLER AND LESS
'EPIC'. THIS VISUAL WAS EXPLORING THE
SIZE RELATIONSHIPS AND ALSO ASKING
WHAT WOULD THE SHED'S HOME BASE
BE? A VERY DIFFICULT PROBLEM, LATER
SOLVED BY STUART'S FANTASTIC WOODEN
HILL. THE FLOATING ORB WAS MY
PITCH FOR THE OBSCURUS — A DARK
MALEVOLENT MOON. I WAS THE ONLY
ONE WHO AGREED. **9**

NEWT'S SHED / DP

⬆ **NEWT IN THE SHED** Newt looks out from the shed to the creature environments – his shed is the centre of his world. **DP**

⬅ **NEWT'S SHED** Newt's shed rests on an artificial 'dune' made of wood. The final set looked like something you would find installed in the Tate Modern's Turbine Hall in London. **DP**

EARLY IMAGE OF THE ENVIRONMENTS One of the first images that I did for Newt's case showed how the environments' individual weather systems would leak from one habitat into another. Rain-filled clouds drift from a warm environment before falling as snow in a frozen one. This also demonstrates Newt's use of an artificial 'sun' and 'moon', which he might use to wake the creatures up or put them to sleep. **DP**

BILLYWIG STINGS Billywig stings are a useful ingredient in potion-making. The tails or stings are valuable and delicate and have been stored carefully in this jar by Newt in order to preserve their potent essence until he needs them. **MS**

DRAGON HIDE GLOVES Wearing dragon hide gloves is an essential safety measure for any witch, wizard or No-Maj who is handling sharp-toothed, poisonous or otherwise dangerous plants and creatures. The hide is naturally fire-proof and impervious so is perfect material for a hardwearing protective glove. **MS**

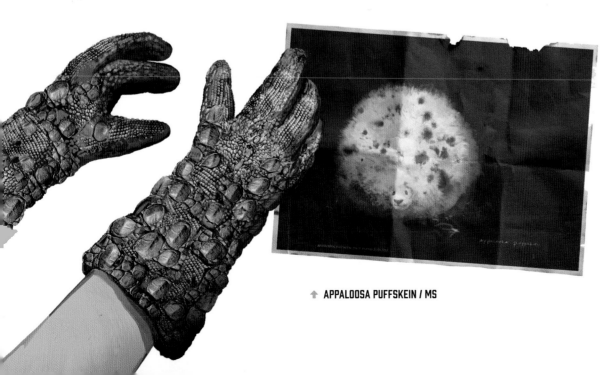

APPALOOSA PUFFSKEIN / MS

→ **THE ENVIRONMENTS AS SEEN FROM ABOVE** Here, all the environments that the actors would physically interact with are laid out as they would be built on the sound stage. Partially built, of course – there isn't a sound stage in existence that would fit all of it in. **DP**

→ **EARLY IDEA FOR NEWT'S SHED** What is Newt's shed on? This early idea (*inset*) imagined it on a floating rock like a child's self-righting roly-poly toy. It might add an interesting swaying motion but also a lot of aggravation. Stuart and I both voted for Newt's shed not to be on anything – better to have it exist wherever he needed it to exist. **DP**

→ **FLOOR PLAN OF THE SHED / SCR**

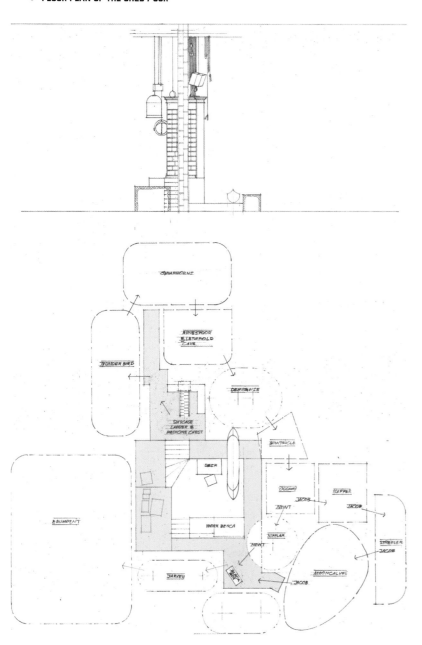

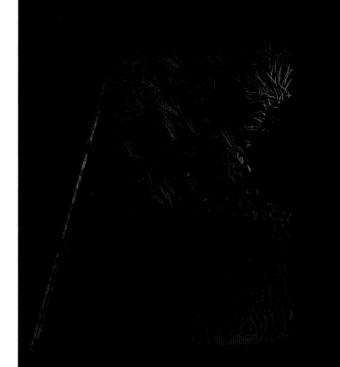

4
THE FANTASTIC BEASTS

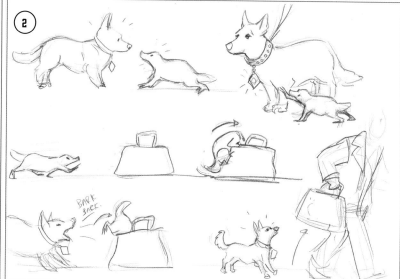

ROUGH SKETCHES EXPLORING THE POTENTIAL FOR THE NIFFLER IN A BANK ENVIRONMENT AND DESCRIBING HIS CHARACTER:

1 Here is the Niffler travelling at bag level. He hasn't yet finished with one thing when he sees the next object of desire. He's quite distracted in that sense. The purse felt like a funny prop to show his absolute focus and interest as he wrestles to retrieve its contents. As the clasp gives way the money pops out and his heart skips a beat as the money shoots out ahead of him.

2 We thought an encounter with a dog would be funny as the Niffler is meeting a sort of equal. It also helps showcase that he has a clear choice in the face of certain danger. The dog can easily bite off his head but the pendant is very attractive. How far is the Niffler willing to go? He is then chased away by the dog and hides in someone's bag, which is then picked up and carried away. I was interested in the idea that the Niffler travels around the bank, evading Newt by good fortune as the wizard struggles to capture him.

3 The Niffler's unstoppable opportunism was inspired by the honey badger, extremely tenacious member of the weasel family that lives in South Africa. Honey badgers stop at nothing to accomplish their goals. They are incredibly resourceful and use other objects to help them get to a tough spot. In this sketch we explored the use of an umbrella to help the Niffler fulfill his need to reach the lady's hat. We were trying to keep the use of props within the realm of animalistic behaviour and avoid anthropomorphism at all costs. Here we also explored the use of the tongue as a way of stealthily retrieving objects.

4 In this sketch we have the Niffler lying in wait behind a man's jacket ready to snatch his pocket watch. Also we wondered if the Niffler might go unnoticed wrapped around a lady's neck disguised as her scarf. All of my sketches in this book were a quick way to think about actions and gags that can be entertaining.

5 Further exploration of tongue use that was later dismissed. We were trying to imagine ways that the Niffler might move around the bank undetected. In this image we see the Niffler being unwittingly plunged into a janitor's bucket with a mop. In this way he would have the good fortune of escaping Newt's clutches by being wheeled across the bank. The handle of the mop is also a useful prop for climbing up to a higher level. **PG**

⬆ **EARLY DESIGN FOR THE NIFFLER** A beady eyed Niffler on a branch clasping coins. **RB**

⬅⬅ **ALTERNATIVE DESIGN FOR THE OCCAMY IN FLIGHT** This introduces an exotic colour scheme to the creature. **RB**

⬅ **EARLY DESIGN FOR THE NIFFLER** Up close and looking sneaky. **RB**

⬆ **EARLY DESIGN FOR THE NIFFLER** The Niffler's big, prehensile nose is ideal for sniffing out shiny objects. **RB**

⬇ **EARLY DESIGN FOR THE NIFFLER** A sly-looking version. **RB**

⬆➡ **THE NIFFLER** David Yates had seen some platypus footage and really liked the way they moved, so these concepts – sculpted 3D models with a little painting over them – are playing with the proportions of the Niffler's features (nose, legs etc.) as well as the idea that its pouch was a large purse-like a tail. We also tried using small feathers instead of fur. **PC**

↓ **THE NIFFLER** A very early attempt, sculpted in ZBrush. **PC**

A SERIES OF TUNNELS, WHICH IS THE NIFFLER'S LAIR This is very interesting to travel through, but not so interesting to look at from outside. So we thought it would be good to combine them with something much more colourful and exotic: the butterfly leaf tree. **DP**

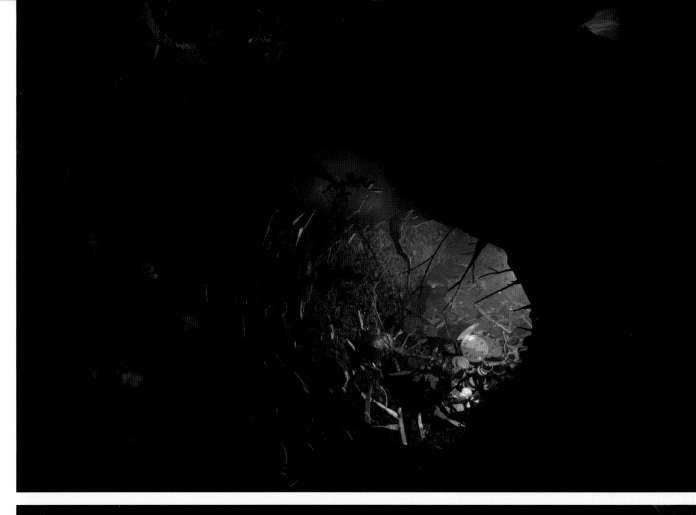

THE NIFFLER ENVIRONMENT Car hood ornament, a gold watch, a brass tap: as long as it is shiny it is valuable to the Niffler. **DP**

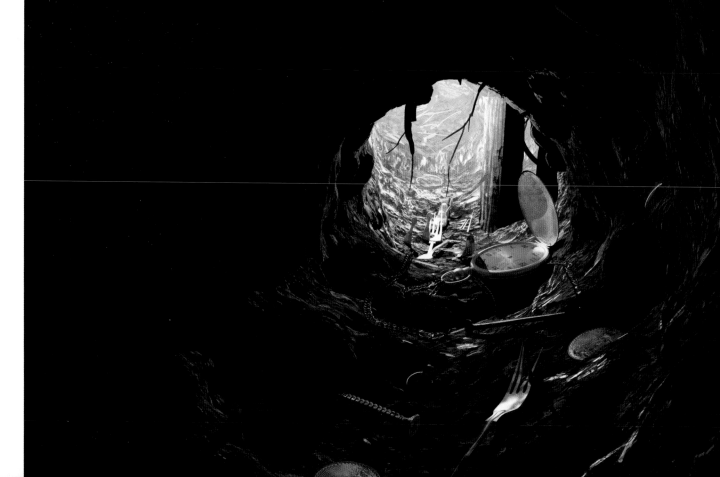

THE NIFFLER ENVIRONMENT Evidence of the Niffler – like finding shiny objects in a magpie nest. **DP**

'A LOOK AT THE NIFFLER STASHING GOLD IN HIS POUCH. THIS WAS MOSTLY EXPLORATIONS OF THE NIFFLER'S COAT, TRYING OUT DOWNY HAIR IN COMPARISON WITH A MORE FEATHERED LOOK.'

THE NIFFLER / AB

↑ **THE MURTLAP** This is a photorealistic render I made for one of my sketches for the Murtlap [below]. At this stage, the creature looks like a mix between an alligator, turtle and a rat. The idea behind the image was to explore its textural appearance in a proper lighting condition. **AV**

➡ **THE MURTLAP** I only produced one of these Murtlaps: I suppose there's not a lot of possibilities for a rat-like creature with a sea anemone on its back. **PC**

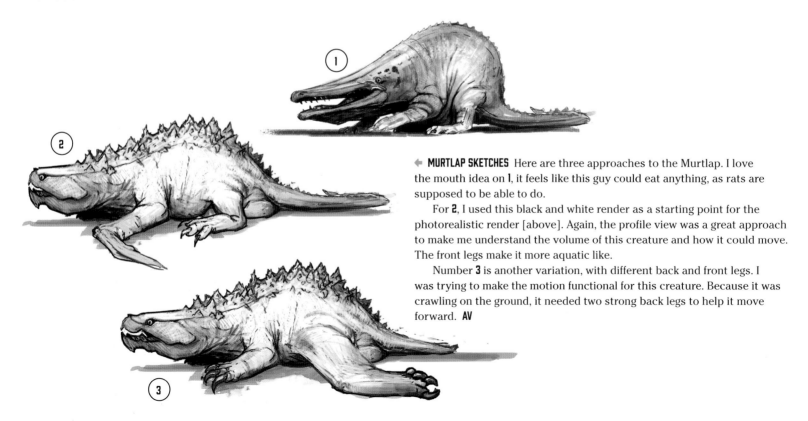

⬅ **MURTLAP SKETCHES** Here are three approaches to the Murtlap. I love the mouth idea on **1**, it feels like this guy could eat anything, as rats are supposed to be able to do.

   For **2**, I used this black and white render as a starting point for the photorealistic render [above]. Again, the profile view was a great approach to make me understand the volume of this creature and how it could move. The front legs make it more aquatic like.

   Number **3** is another variation, with different back and front legs. I was trying to make the motion functional for this creature. Because it was crawling on the ground, it needed two strong back legs to help it move forward. **AV**

◄ **THE GRAPHORN ENCLOSURE** We wanted the Graphorns to be hidden at first – the sound of their hooves on the loose rocks would be the first sign of their existence. **DP**

THE GRAPHORN ENCLOSURE This is the second environment that we visit after that of the Thunderbird. I wanted to immediately break any expectation the audience might have of what the 'rules' for the environments might be. The Thunderbird environment had an animated painted backing, the Graphorn environment floats in a star-studded black void. Similar visual 'language' of rough, worn planks and posts with sand and rocks keeps it all aesthetically consistent. I also liked the strangeness of a brightly lit landscape against a black sky. **DP**

THE GRAPHORN / PC

↑ **THE GRAPHORN** loved the description of the Graphorn in J.K. Rowling's book and wanted to do it justice, but I also wanted it to be distinct from the Erumpent. In these sculpted 3D models I made it slimmer and more shapely, to avoid it looking too much like an Ibex; I then added the tentacle beard, which I thought it could use to catch termites or ants. **PC**

➡ THE GRAPHORN Paul Catling created the original design for the Graphorn, which I personally think looked fantastic. I was then asked to redesign its head and neck, and flesh out its finer details overall. The biggest design change to the head was adding multiple horns.

We approached this like a real animal. It had to move like a cat but be big and powerful like an elephant or rhino. It had to be intimidating at first glance but also endearing and nurturing with strong family bonds. Finally, it needed to have adapted its colour and skin type to fit into its desert environment.

A couple of concept paintings were done resulting in a new design that helped our 3D model and texturing department. **RJ**

⬆ THE GRAPHORN I wanted to illustrate the book's description of the Graphorn having 'an extremely aggressive nature' by keeping its head low, permanently in ramming mode, its shoulders massive and unyielding yet with a slim, almost athletic rear end that can accelerate, cheetah-like, propelling its huge bulk and sharp horns towards its foe. **PC**

← **THE RUNESPOOR** The Runespoor was supposed to be a regular-sized snake and everyone seemed fine with that until about mid-production when Christian Manz asked me to redesign it from scratch and to make it "fantastic" and "huge". I had full creative licence and it was an honour for me to have the chance to contribute to the film as creature designer. **ABR**

↑ **THE RUNESPOOR / PC**

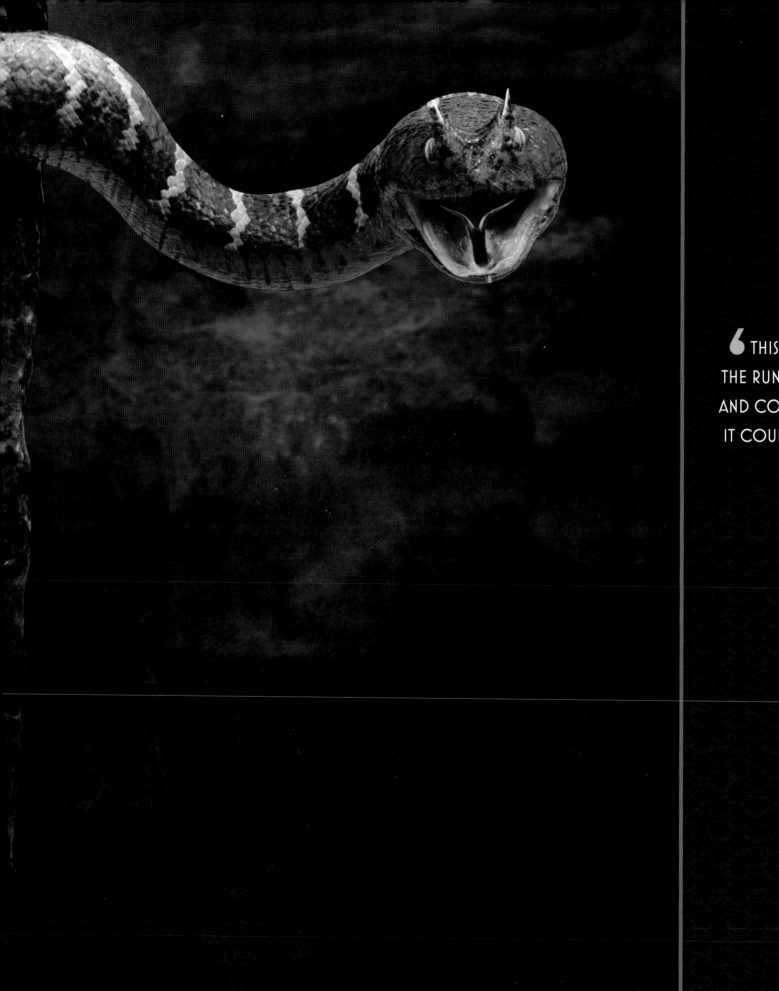

'THIS IMAGE WAS RESOLVING THE RUNESPOOR'S SKIN TEXTURES AND COLOUR, AS WELL AS HOW IT COULD LIVE AND CRAWL ON STALACTITES.'

THE RUNESPOOR / AV

↑ **THE BOWTRUCKLE** A combination of beauty, strength and danger: that's what I pursued when creating this concept. **MK**

↑ **THE BOWTRUCKLE** I drew this version in anticipation of feedback from the art director. I tried to make it scary because the previous version was too appealing. **MK**

← **THE BOWTRUCKLE** This was my attempt to make the Bowtruckle cuter by using, rather randomly, the appearance of a seahorse. **PC**

→ **EARLY BOWTRUCKLE DESIGN** His bark is worse than his bite... **RB**

← IDEA FOR THE BOWTRUCKLE ENVIRONMENT I did this when I thought it might be more of a fairy tale forest. DP

↑ THE BOWTRUCKLE ENVIRONMENT We come to this habitat just after the Occamy's bamboo environment. I felt it would get lost if it was another forest so solved that by making this one much more sculptural and also to have it float and turn. The trees are like characters themselves. An earlier version was more bonsai in appearance until David Yates commented that 'bonsai' is too 'ordinarily extraordinary'. DP

⬆ **EARLY BOWTRUCKLE DESIGN** This version looks more green and leafy. **RB**

⬆ **EARLY BOWTRUCKLE DESIGN** This is his attempt to blend in with a tree. **RB**

➡ **THE BOWTRUCKLE** With this one, on the other hand, I took the insect side too far and it was rightly pointed out to me – who on Earth would want a gnarly insect man poking around inside your ears? **PC**

⬆ **THE BOWTRUCKLE** Here I used an insect as a base with a random mouse head to make its mantis-like body a little more friendly. No one was fooled. **PC**

⬆ **THE BOWTRUCKLE** This was well liked. I think it has a reasonable balance between twigs and insect. **PC**

⬆ **THE BOWTRUCKLE** This character was interesting for me, but unfortunately I spent a couple of hours on it. When I was asked to proceed with the next, I was not able to deeply explore it. **MK**

⬇ **SERIES OF BOWTRUCKLE DESIGNS** I worked with Martin Macrae on these creatures; using Pickett as a reference I did a series of silhouettes to get a feel for some different characters. Once we had those approved we took them in to a more photo-real finish where Martin did the majority of work to get them looking more realistic, using lots of sapling reference to get the surface texture right. **DB**

⬆ **THE BOWTRUCKLE** When trying to create something unique and never seen before, sometimes you have to try less obvious ideas before coming back to the fact that a 'twig man' should look like a man made out of twigs. **PC**

➡ **ONE OF THE FINAL DESIGNS FOR THE BOWTRUCKLE** Many artists worked on this piece. Getting the character right was quite tricky. The Bowtruckle needed to be friendly but also a little formidable. **MM**

↟ **THE BOWTRUCKLE** These designs were based on the work of another artist. They use the language of a silver birch tree to create the features and expressions of the face. The asymmetry makes it seem as if the creature grew organically from the tree rather than following a set plan like a human or other animal. **BK**

↟ **THE BOWTRUCKLE** This one is based on a fallen leaf. I've always loved the way leaves curl in on themselves as they dry out becoming like insect shells. **BK**

↞ **THE BOWTRUCKLE** In this concept I was playing around with leaf shapes for the body. I wanted the audience to see the leaf first and at second glance see the Bowtruckle, like camouflage. **SR**

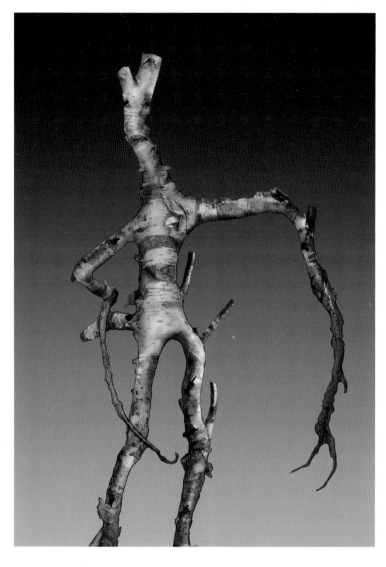

THE BOWTRUCKLE More explorations of the Bowtruckle. PC

THE BOWTRUCKLE One of the many variations I did. It was a team effort to work on this creature. At this stage I was exploring a lot with eye variations in order to make this head believable. I took the idea of insect's eyes to avoid anything too stylized. AV

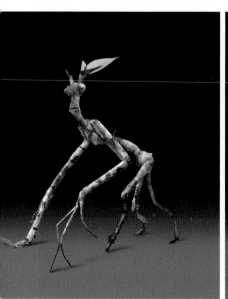

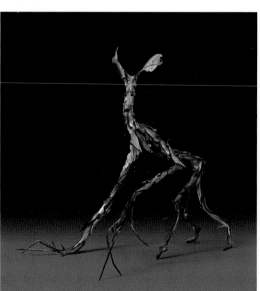

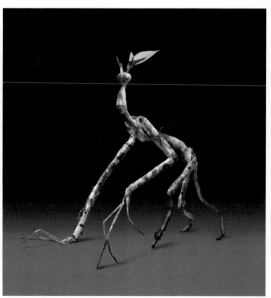

← **THE MOONCALF PLANET** This is made of a broken sphere held together with cables to bolster Newt's not-quite-right magical construction. **DP**

→ **THE MOONCALF PLANET** Stuart was really keen to keep the 'segmented orange' feel – like Sydney Opera House – so there is a strong contrast between the rough, bumpy, eroded outer surface and the sharp, clean, sliced inner surface. **DP**

↓ **SKETCHES OF MOONCALVES** Drawing these was a way to become familiar with Paul's concept, to try to understand the Mooncalf from the point of view of construction, motion and character. **PG**

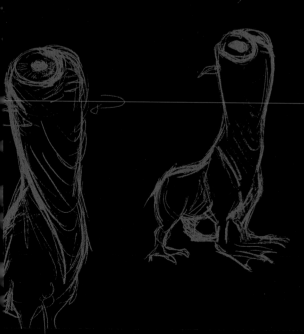

↑ **THE MOONCALF PLANET** Newt's magical powers enabled him to float the Mooncalf planetoid but not bring it back to earth. This is what the windlass is for – just enough mechanical ingenuity to help him out, but he is no Heath Robinson. The wooden 'wave' platform is inspired by early twentieth-century wooden rollercoasters. I wanted it to feel as if it had been partially created with the sweep of a wand then finished with hammers and nails. **DP**

↑ **THE MOONCALF** My second attempt at a Mooncalf, the first being more goat-like. It was described as having eyes on top of its head, which gives the notion that the Mooncalf had somehow evolved solely to stare at the moon, so I thought I'd strip away any features that didn't fit that idea. **PC**

↑ **THE MOONCALF** The barn owl face didn't make it with the Demiguise so I tried to shoehorn it into the Mooncalf design. Luckily people had already warmed to the earlier concept. **PC**

MOONCALF DUNG To design the droppings of any magical creature is a bizarre and exciting brief. We considered the characteristics and habits of the moon-worshipping miniature calves, and gave the droppings a size and texture we felt naturally befitted them, along with a distribution in the meadow which would give the planet a lived-in look. The 'pats' are created when the creatures come out at night and stare at the full moon, clustering their excretions in one area so as to protect the grass from becoming sour. Much like a cowpat, the surface is pitted and irregular, faintly resembling the craters of the moon. The silver dusted surface is a small clue to the superpower of the dung when used as a fertiliser on plants and vegetables. Hence Newt's barrow full to the brim in this visual. **MS**

THE MOONCALF The Mooncalf is an adorable creature. Designing realistic facial features while preserving the cartoon proportions that gave the Mooncalf its endearing look was a fine balancing act. And I had the chance to work with my VFX supervisor Arnaud Brisebois on this image. **SC**

⬆ **THE OBSCURUS HABITAT** A frozen environment to contrast with the hot, dusty Erumpent habitat just next door. A good home for the Obscurus. This was painted over a frame from an animation that also showed how the mechanical moon opens and closes to show its quarter, half and full phases. **OP**

➡ **THE OBSCURUS** This was a concept I was asked to do showing the Obscurus trapped in a box or tablet shape. Here, we see the face pushing through the surface. **DB**

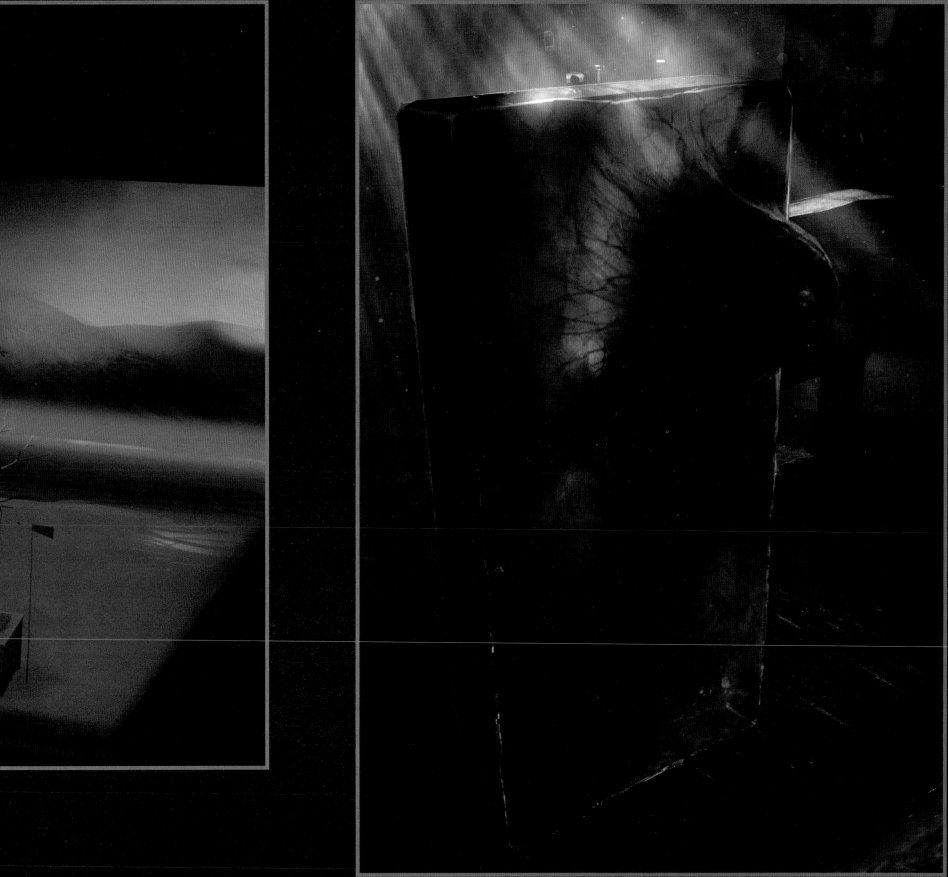

ABANDONED ENVIRONMENT IDEA We were very keen to keep the environments slightly 'arch' and theatrical. They have a reality akin to the panoramic backings in the New York Natural History Museum, but instead of including elements to support the illusion of reality we looked for elements to hint at the un-reality. In this case the rocks and trees are quite 'staged': a little too perfectly placed.

This image also demonstrated an abandoned idea, which was to have the habitats appear as 'ghosts' in each world in turn, seen in their background. Newt's shed existing where he needed it to be and Newt walking or jumping from one habitat to another. No need for a home base because home is where your shed is. **DP**

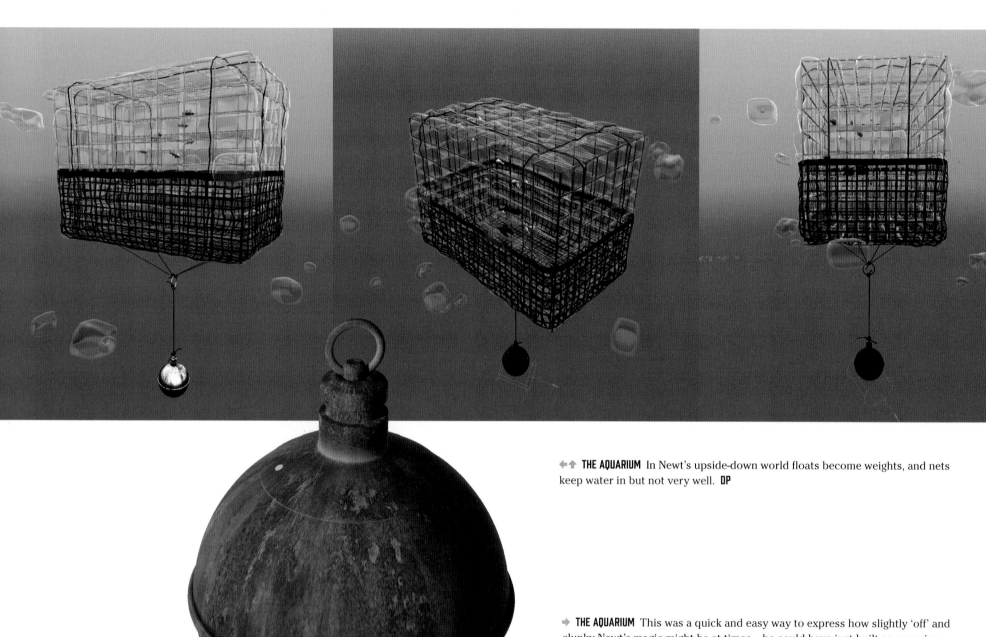

← ↑ THE AQUARIUM In Newt's upside-down world floats become weights, and nets keep water in but not very well. **DP**

→ THE AQUARIUM This was a quick and easy way to express how slightly 'off' and clunky Newt's magic might be at times – he could have just built an aquarium but instead he magics the water in to a block; but it doesn't quite work and some of the sea creatures float off. **DP**

→ **THE ERUMPENT ENVIRONMENT** Evidence of the Erumpent's escape – with giant bugs swarming in the shafts of light. **DP**

← **THE ERUMPENT ENVIRONMENT** The Erumpent environment backing is magical like the Thunderbird one, but made to look like it is painted on sheer muslin rather than canvas so it is translucent and allows the light to pour through the boards. **DP**

↑ **THE ERUMPENT ENVIRONMENT** Inspired in part by the raptor cages in the original *Jurassic Park* – you know something dangerous is in there but you can't quite make it out. **DP**

← **THE ERUMPENT ENVIRONMENT** From this angle we can see what Newt can't see (yet): the Erumpent has smashed out of the back of her habitat. **DP**

THE ERUMPENT IN ITS HABITAT Here I have placed Rob Bliss's Erumpent sculpts into my creature habitat design. This is not strictly correct, as the large creatures would not share a habitat – the herbivores wouldn't last very long if they did. **DP**

↑ **VERY EARLY ERUMPENT DESIGN** I'm not sure why but I apparently thought it was the size of about twenty buses stacked on top of each other. **RB**

↑ **ANOTHER EARLY OVERSIZED ERUMPENT DESIGN / RB**

↓ **ALTERNATIVE ERUMPENT DESIGN WITH A TOUCH OF COLOUR / RB**

↓ **THE ERUMPENT / RB**

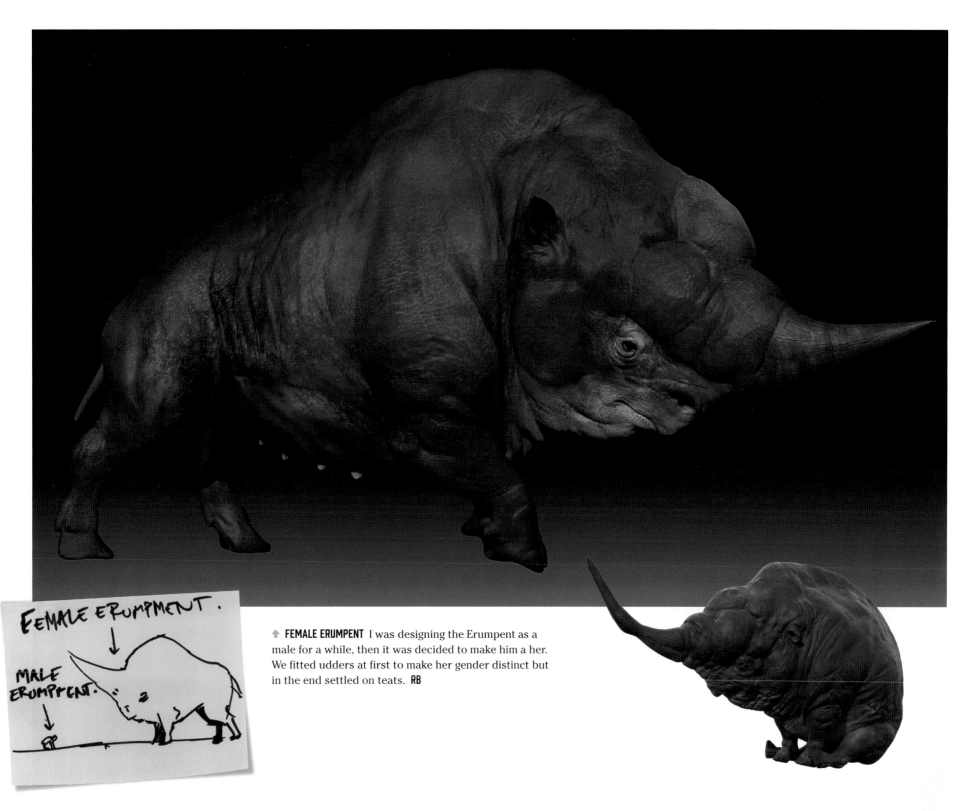

⬆ **FEMALE ERUMPENT** I was designing the Erumpent as a male for a while, then it was decided to make him a her. We fitted udders at first to make her gender distinct but in the end settled on teats. **RB**

⬆ **MALE ERUMPENT** Sexual dimorphism is the term for the physical differences between males and females of any species. Sometimes it is expressed in extreme ways. How could we have it occur in magical creatures so as to be humorous and entertaining? In this gag Jacob might ponder over a small and feeble looking beast. 'What's this one called?' he might ask Newt. 'Ah, that's the male Erumpent.' **PG**

⬆ **MALE ERUMPENT** Here is the Erumpent male, smaller than the female, pining for his mate. Small enough to be bossed around whilst still big enough to crush your house. **RB**

↑ **EARLY ERUMPENT SKETCH** This was the first piece that I did for *Fantastic Beasts*. I was trying to get a sense of a big playful creature, with elements of a bull terrier dog, manatee and a beetle. **DB**

↑ **THE ERUMPENT** Another approach. This one has more of a bulldog feel to him, I was testing the idea of a semi-transparent pouch on his back that would reveal the liquid it creates inside. **DB**

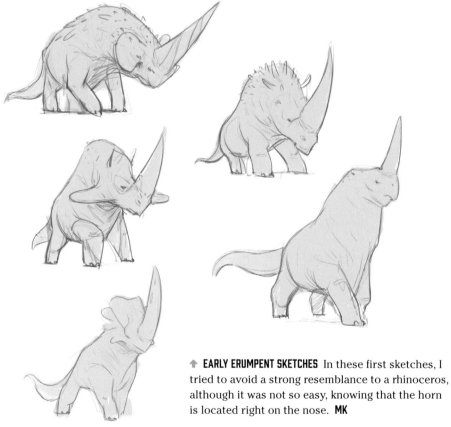

↑ **EARLY ERUMPENT SKETCHES** In these first sketches, I tried to avoid a strong resemblance to a rhinoceros, although it was not so easy, knowing that the horn is located right on the nose. **MK**

↑ **ALTERNATIVE ERUMPENT DESIGN** So maybe these guys are so sad, they did not pass the audition. It happens... **MK**

⬆ **THE ERUMPENT** A futher exploration of the Erumpent. **DB**

⬆ **THE ERUMPENT** This idea was heavily influenced by the African hippo. I love the texture of these creatures. I combined this with a more whimsical, spherical silhouette. **DB**

⬇ **SKETCHES FOR THE HIPPO-INSPIRED ERUMPENT** Again really trying to get a sense of character from the poses. **DB**

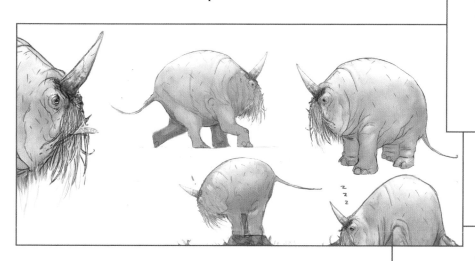

⬆ **EARLY ERUMPENT SKETCH** This shows how the Erumpent might inflate the liquid filled pouch on its back. **DB**

➡ **EARLY ERUMPENT SKETCHES** These were great fun, just trying to a get a sense of how the Erumpent might move or interact with the film's characters. **DB**

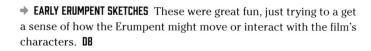

THE ERUMPENT Here I tried to make the Erumpent a little cuter, using the American bison shape, but the colour scheme was deemed too alien. **PC**

THE ERUMPENT I thought this was fun for the Erumpent: a giant crab-rhino thing; but it's supposed to be a creature we can feel sympathy for. **PC**

THE ERUMPENT With this one I again took the rough profile of an American bison and wildly exaggerated the chest. It made me giggle imagining it running – its tiny little front legs scurrying desperately, trying to keep up with the galloping rear legs. However, the lack of proper face gave it little personality. **PC**

THE ERUMPENT I drew this image to show a dramatic moment at the zoo in Central Park. The Erumpent, which is on heat, is crashing against a wall, destroying everything in her path and threatening the small hippos around her. The dramatic action in the scene has been pushed by an intense lighting cutting through the frame and casting strong dark shadows, while the atmosphere has been enriched by dust and debris. Ultimately the aggressive pose of the Erumpent conveys the full dramatic power of the situation. **FC**

⬆ **THE ERUMPENT** This creature combines the sturdy power of a rhinoceros with the ethereal strangeness of a jellyfish. **BK**

⬅ **ERUMPENT SKETCH** This time its horn is filled with its explosive glowing liquid. **SR**

⬇ **THE ERUMPENT** I came on to *Fantastic Beasts and Where to Find Them* during the middle of the design stage. A lot of the early ideas had been sketched out and Rob Bliss had laid a solid base for the Erumpent. This was an experiment with scent glands along her back. This would give the audience a visual cue that she was in heat. **SR**

↑ **SKETCH FOR THE NUNDU ENVIRONMENT** This was for me to explore what I was going to explore, complete with a snail completing the world's slowest loop-the-loop. **DP**

→ **THE NUNDU ENVIRONMENT** Stuart loved the concept that the Nundus and a snail-like beast existed so close to each other but that the Nundu would have no idea that these dark mysterious creatures are just beneath its feet. A metaphor for the Muggles and the wizarding world. Of course I pretended *that* was what I was going for. **DP**

THE NUNDU The Nundu is an exceptionally dangerous beast. For this version I looked at the hoods of medieval executioners and the bodies of hairless beasts. **BK**

THE NUNDU Another idea for the Nundu referenced spitting cobras and puffer fish and the way they expand when threatened. I tried to apply this behaviour to the creature's lion-like mane. **BK**

➡ ➡ **A NUNDU IN BOTH ITS NORMAL STATE AND ITS INFLATED ONE** The main image was inspired by the puffer fish. **SR**

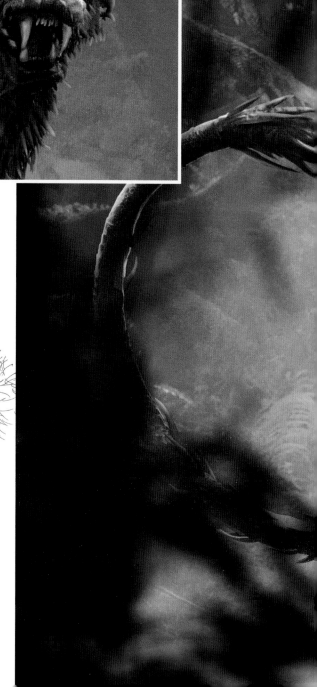

➡ **SKETCH FOR NUNDU HABITAT** I liked the idea of the environment being stored like a theatre set with the trees and rocks obeying their local magical physics (i.e. they don't fall off when stacked sideways). But I didn't develop this idea beyond the sketch. **OP**

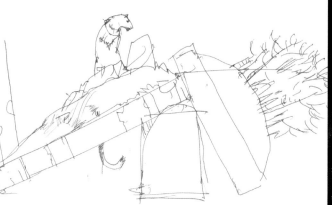

⬅ **THE NUNDU** The Nundu is described has having breath that reeks of disease. I liked the idea that this contamination would spread throughout the body so the whole creature was covered in mould and fungi. **BK**

A LITTLE INSECT BIODOME THAT MIGHT FLOAT ABOUT RANDOMLY IN THE ENVIRONMENTS It was decided it might be a bit cruel. DP

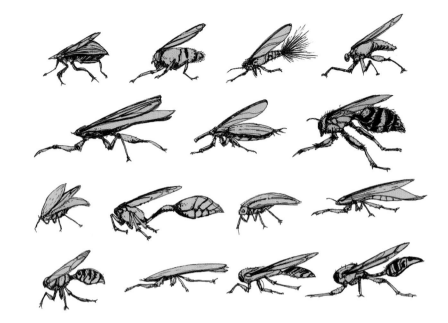
⬆ EARLY BILLYWIG SKETCHES With these I wanted to explore as many body shape variations as I could. The profile view was a great starting point as I had the possibility to look for an iconic silhouette in order to build a strong signature look. Going in different directions would then give me a more creative result. AV

⬇ THE BILLYWIG / PC

THE FWOOPER This was probably the easiest concept I had to do. I just looked at J.K. Rowling's drawing in the book and redrew it. I did add a bit of owl, though. **PC**

THE FWOOPER This is one of the characters that was approved before I started making sketches. **MK**

THE GLOW WORM The design of the Glow Worm required a lot of research and experiments. The challenge here was to create a believable insect anatomy while mimicking incandescent tungsten filaments found in standard light bulbs. **SC**

THE SHRIMP CREATURE The one was a lot of fun. I was asked to look at different types of transparent sea creatures to help capture some of its more grotesque otherworldly qualities. The tentacles were actually inspired by the bodies of hagfish which I thought where creepier somehow than traditional tentacles found on squid or octopuses. **DB**

THE SHRIMP CREATURE This version of the creature is a cross between a carpet mite and a shrimp. The 'eye' opens to reveal itself a rather nasty beak. **BK**

THE SHRIMP CREATURE I wanted this creature to have the heft and dangling limbs of a large toddler, while at the same time being rather disgusting. **BK**

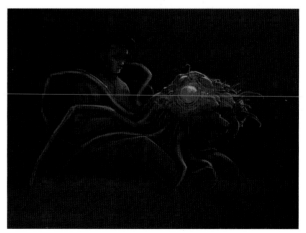

THE SHRIMP CREATURE Though a spider's speed and movements are usually rather scary I though they could also denote friendliness and enthusiasm. **BK**

⬆ **DESIGN FOR THE DUNG BEETLE** Finding the balance between a believable, fantastical insect and a relatable character was fun. **SR**

THE DUNG BEETLE Here I was trying to create a beetle that masquerades as a flower. The open version looks much more interesting. **MK**

THE DUNG BEETLE This beetle uses its mandibles like a pair of outside callipers to assess the size of its dung ball. **BK**

THE DUNG BEETLE This idea came from watching a dog trying to carry a large ball in its mouth and always dropping it. **BK**

THE DUNG BEETLE I liked the idea of giving its industrious qualities to something really big. **BK**

↓ **DOXY SKETCHES** I was only able to work on the Doxy for two days, after which I took on another character. I really liked the idea of black fairies. **MK**

→ AN EARLY DOXY DESIGN / RB

↑ **THE DOXY** In this embodiment of the Doxy, I combined the overall colour of the gorilla and wings of black beetles. **MK**

↓ **THE DOXY** In this version I also used the black fur and bluish iridescence of beetles. **MK**

→ **THE DOXY** Here is a design where I tried to blend some characteristics of a tree frog with a moth. It was based on an early frog-like sketch that Ben Kovar had done and which I was asked to develop further. I loved the idea of the Doxy using its ears as wings: it added a nice bit of humour to the creature. **SR**

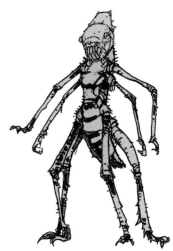

DOXY?
NEEDS IDEA

⬆ **DOXY SKETCH / PG**

⬆ **THE DOXY** This Doxy's ears can make it either sweet or scary. I liked the idea of a creature whose aggression was out of all proportion to its size and appearance. **BK**

⬇ **EARLY SKETCHES FOR THE DOXY** I decided to draw them as insects, so they could exist in Nature. I wanted to avoid any human limb-joints to get away from the idea of the fairy. **AV**

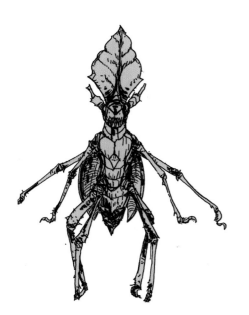
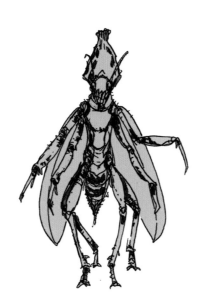
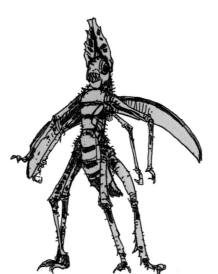

↑ **THE DIRICAWL** This design is based on a Dodo, its magical nature masked by its mundane appearance. **BK**

← **THE DIRICAWL** These are various options for the Diricawl, a very cute bird, with a variety of colour. **MK**

↓ **THE DIRICAWL** Though not typical work for me, I really had fun coming up with different methods of extinction of this bird. **MK**

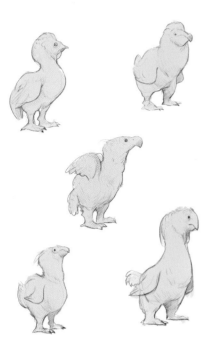

↑ **DIRICAWL SKETCHES** The outline of the Diricawl, an ancient, extinct bird that resembles the Dodo. Despite this similarity I tried to make a slightly different version. **MK**

↓→ **THE DIRICAWL** I tried to use an interesting combination of colours here in order to avoid any resemblance to a bird in *Alice in Wonderland*. **MK**

THE SWOOPING EVIL IN COCOON FORM This was a more photo-real approach to the Swooping Evil. At the time, I was looking at the early stage of insect pupae for reference as well as some plants and tree seeds. **DB**

SWOOPING EVIL HEAD STUDY After I got an overall feeling for the Swooping Evil I did this to really get a feeling for what the surface of its skin might feel like and how the skull fits under that strange organic hood. **DB**

THE SWOOPING EVIL Working on the Swooping Evil was a real joy. I remember thinking the description of the creature was fantastic. I was looking at various different butterfly species as I liked the idea of this juxtaposing with that terrifying animal-like skull! **DB**

SWOOPING EVIL MOTION STUDY This was a really quick study I did to get a feeling of how the Swooping Evil might open up after it is thrown in the air. **DB**

DEMIGUISE AND OCCAMY NESTS How do you show an 'absent' creature was a recurring challenge in this story. Two big challenges in this example, where the Demiguise nest hovers above the giant Occamy one, guarding it. This was inspired by something you might see in the Sculpture Park in Yorkshire. **DP**

REJECTED CONCEPT FOR A CREATURE Although this was rejected, it was very interesting to combine plant and reptile. **MK**

ARTIFICIAL 'SUN' Newt moves this around the environment and it throws interesting shadows. **DP**

OCCAMY EGG / MS

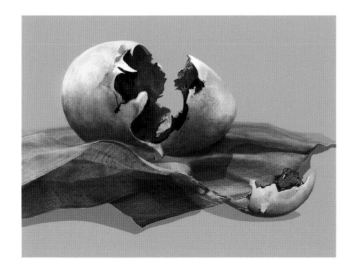

THE DEMIGUISE NEST Stuart was worried that this might look too much like a piece of sixties furniture – the solution was to ask the props department to create the Demiguise nest purely by eye, without measuring anything, to make it more organic. The result was something reminiscent of mud wasps' nests and paper-maché masks we made when we were kids.

An example of the idea that concept design is about asking questions not necessarily answering them: I put books in to the Demiguise nest. Can he read? I was told 'probably not' – but maybe he likes picture books. **DP**

⬆ **THE DEMIGUISE** This image shows the Demiguise living in a wild and verdant forest. Here the creature is a mix between a hairy ape and a lemur. **AV**

⬆ **THE DEMIGUISE** This Demiguise was a reaction to David Yates remarking that earlier designs looked less interesting than actual Orangutans. It's basically a monkey with a barn owl face, but I thought it worked probably a bit better than others did so I decided to 'magic it up' a bit. **PC**

➡ **THE DEMIGUISE** This is the magical version. I imagined that its actual body was tiny, hidden in a mass of prehensile fur. Its limbs are made entirely from this fur so they could stretch out to reach distant branches as it swings gracefully through the forest. **PC**

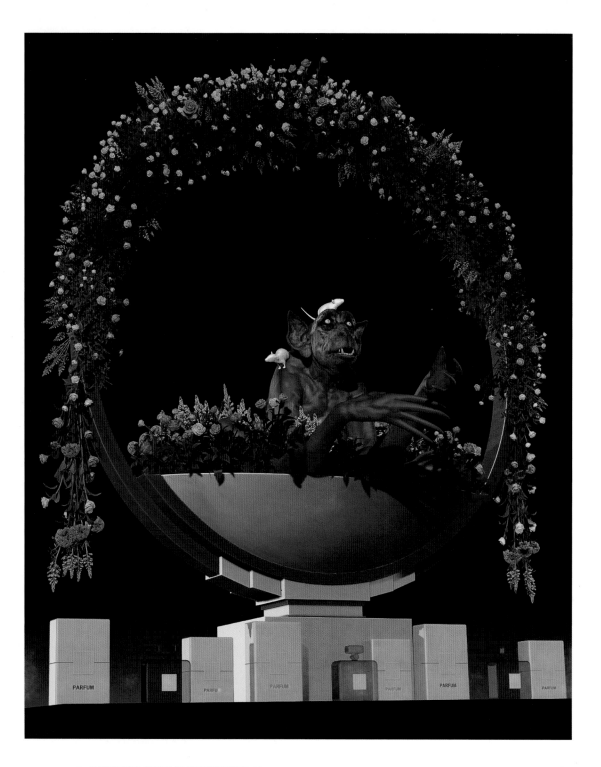

↑ **ALTERNATIVE DESIGN OF THE DEMIGUISE** Here we see it amongst the flowers in the department store. **RB**

➡ **EARLY LEAPING DEMIGUISE** In this early concept I wanted to convey the sense of energy as the Demiguise leaps across the crockery department. **RB**

THE DEMIGUISE During the early stage of the design period, we were looking to the orangutan for a design lead on the appearance of the Demiguise, as we tried to combine the humanity of the ape with his simian agility. Here he is hanging off a lamppost. **RB**

ALTERNATIVE DEMIGUISE DESIGN In this design he is happily focused on a pretty butterfly. **RB**

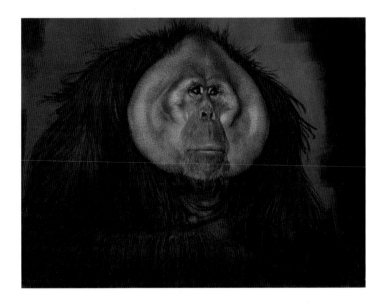

ALTERNATIVE DEMIGUISE DESIGNS These are two further explorations of the Demiguise, of the full body and in close-up. **RB**

"THIS WAS THE IMAGE THAT
DIRECTOR DAVID YATES KEPT
COMING BACK TO AGAIN AND
AGAIN. THOUGH THE DETAILS OF THE
DESIGN WERE NOT QUITE RIGHT, THE
ATTITUDE AND MOOD WAS EXACTLY
WHAT HE WANTED. THIS HAPPENS
A LOT IN CONCEPT DESIGN: A
PARTICULAR IMAGE WILL SNAG IN THE
DIRECTOR'S MIND FOR REASONS HARD
TO PIN DOWN, SO YOU HAVE TO PAY
CLOSE ATTENTION TO IMAGES THEY
COME BACK TO."

A HANDBAG-CLUTCHING DEMIGUISE FEEDING BABY OCCAMIES / RB

FOUR ATTEMPTS AT A DEMIGUISE The first one I really liked (1), but unfortunately the director was less keen so I started doing other options. The second option (2) was closer to what the director had in mind, but still not ideal, so I moved on. Another (3), was more reminiscent of a sloth or lemur and was closer to the final image. Lastly, I did one with a fancy head (4). **MK**

THE FIRST SKETCHES OF THE DEMIGUISE Initially, I tried to make it more playful and perhaps overly humanized. In these cases, I tried to create a character more like a sloth. Once everyone was happy with this view of the Demiguise, I made a side and front view then transported him to the film noir-style scenes. **MK**

THE DEMIGUISE The Demiguise was my favourite character, possibly due to the fact that I worked the longest on it, and almost all my variants the director liked. This is the final approved version. **MK**

↟ **THE DEMIGUISE** We were playing with the expressionistic ways of showing the Demiguise's movement through space. The brief was to come up with a surrealistic tone to this scene. We looked at a lot of film noir, German expressionism and art deco fashion photography where the use of light and shadows is very inventive. We thought that this creature might be able to sneak around the department store via his shadow creating interesting elongating shapes. Perhaps his shadow would operate in contradiction to his own movements. **PG**

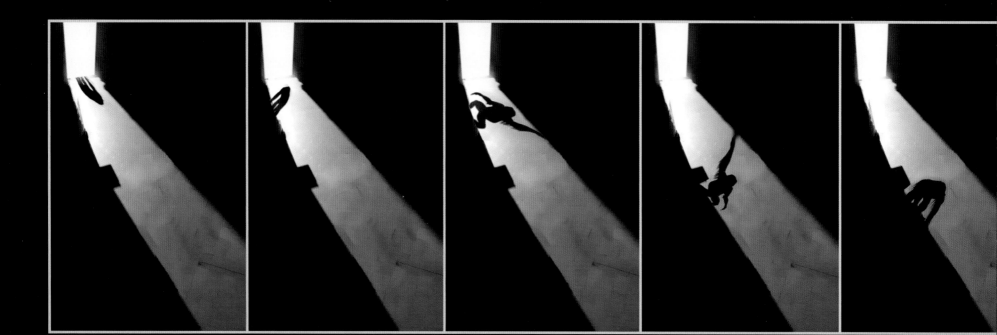

⬇ **CONCEPT SEQUENCE OF THE DEMIGUISE** Pablo asked me to do this to show how the Demiguise might move around using shadows, completely breaking the laws of physics as he goes. **DB**

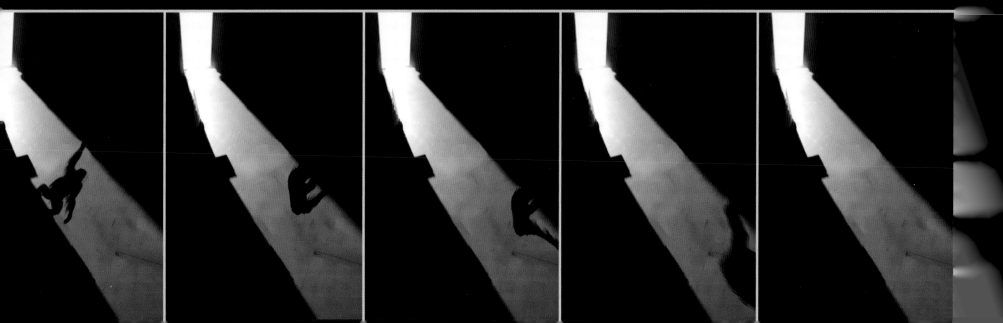

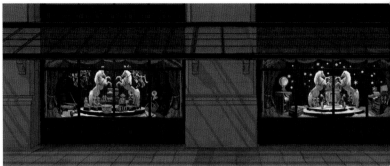

⬇ DEMIGUISE SKETCH Here we were trying to steer away from a monkey yet maintain some sort of simian strength and agility in the upper body. We were looking for a character with the haunted qualities of Nosferatu or Bela Lugosi. A caring old beast with melancholic eyes that just wants to be left alone with the burden of his responsibilities. **PG**

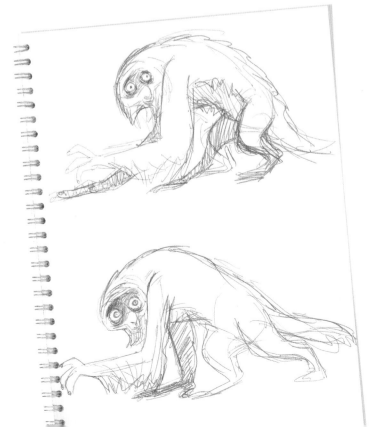

⬆ EVOLUTION OF AN EARLIER SKETCH OF THE DEMIGUISE It was a tricky character to get right, with its long grey hair and wrinkly skin. The Demiguise could come across frail but it is more like a lemur, strong and dexterous when it needs to be. **SR**

THE DEMIGUISE
TRANSFORMING INTO A CHAIR I was trying to get some personality into him. I thought he could be slightly mad or hyperactive, busy collecting things – even when in stealth mode, he can't keep his head still as he searches for something else to pilfer. **PC**

THE DEMIGUISE This was one of a few studies of the Demiguise, trying to get him looking old and wise. A lot of this came from referencing orangutans. **AB**

THE DEMIGUISE A last attempt by me at the Demiguise when opinion was favouring another direction, so I threw in a bit of dog, a slice of cat, a lump of monkey – everything including the kitchen sink! **PC**

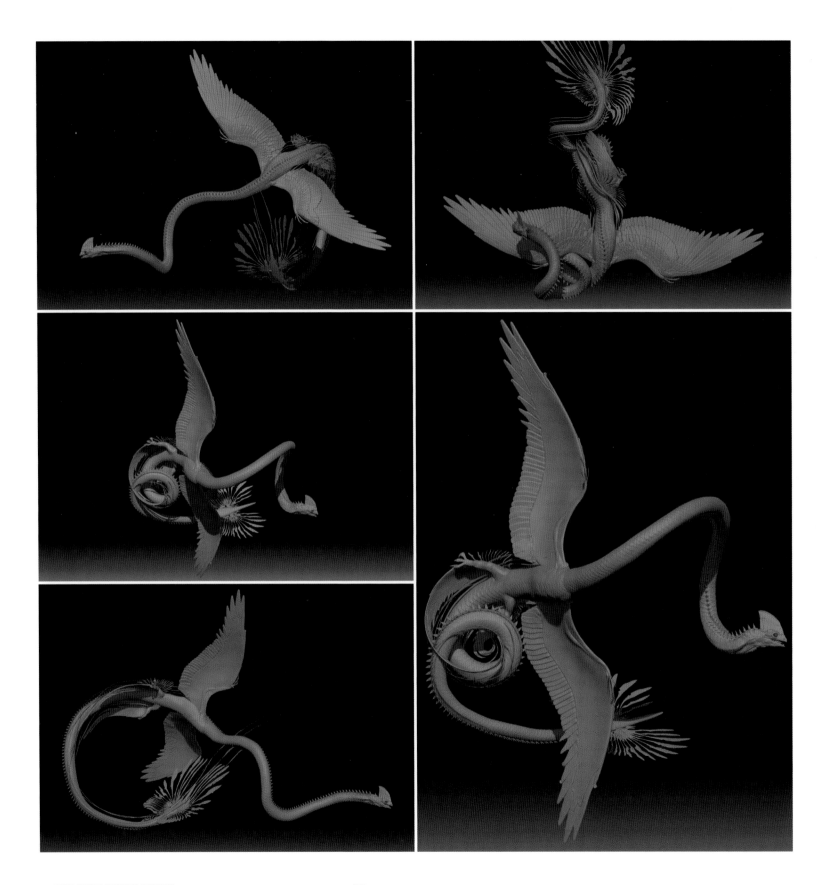

⬆ **VERY EARLY OCCAMY DESIGNS** Working in greyscale at this point. **RB**

↑ **THE OCCAMY ON TOP OF THE DEPARTMENT STORE WITH HER CHICKS** Her colour was much more muted at this stage. **RB**

↑ **BABY OCCAMY** For the baby Occamy we had to show an obvious resemblance to its mother regarding features and colours, but it also needed to look strange and clumsy as a newborn chick. This was a fun one to design and realize. **MM**

↑ **BABY OCCAMY** For this scene we witness the hatching of a baby Occamy. Its shell needed to maintain the same iridescent quality as the feathers of a fully grown Occamy. **MM**

↑ **THE GOLDEN VERSION OF THE SILVER OCCAMY EGG, WHICH WAS NEVER MADE** In the process of designing the silver egg we explored more rounded, smaller, patterned and enamel finishes to try to evoke the script's description of a valuable yet soft silver shell. A palm-sized, duck-egg shape was opted for, with a weathered burnished finish to help give the otherwise precise man-made material a more organic feel. **MS**

↑ **OCCAMY SKETCHES** I did these early on, trying to mix serpentine qualities with that of a bird. **DB**

⬆ **THE OCCAMY** In the story this creature has Asian roots, so I was trying to see how it might look like in its natural environment. **JJ**

⬅ **A SERIES OF QUICK COLOUR STUDIES FOR THE OCCAMY** I did these on top of my 3D models, to see how we might utilize the idea of having a bird with vibrant colours. Still having some American eagle patterns, I was trying to introduce something that would create a nice contrast such as a bright green iridescence (**1**). Exploring an idea of mixing in some snake patterns and shapes. The cobra was a main reference for this one (**3**). One idea was to have her wings attached to the legs, which I thought could create an interesting visual when she flies (**5**). **JJ**

⬆ **THE OCCAMY** The Occamy is all about illusion. I liked the idea of the wings being translucent, like stained glass windows, and the creature just a dark shape between them. **BK**

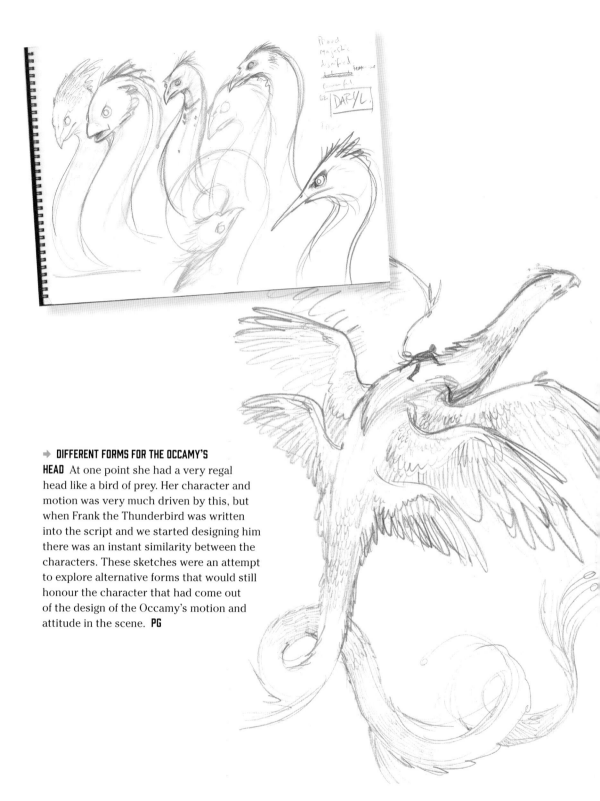

DIFFERENT FORMS FOR THE OCCAMY'S HEAD At one point she had a very regal head like a bird of prey. Her character and motion was very much driven by this, but when Frank the Thunderbird was written into the script and we started designing him there was an instant similarity between the characters. These sketches were an attempt to explore alternative forms that would still honour the character that had come out of the design of the Occamy's motion and attitude in the scene. **PG**

THE OCCAMY IN FLIGHT I was mainly involved in the early stages of the Occamy's development. My task was to experiment with an idea of having multiple wings and the flight mechanics of this creature. The main challenge was to make her elegant both in flight and on the ground, so I was playing with an idea of using wings as legs as she walks on the ground. This is one of those projects where starting with a very rough 3D gestural sculpture is the best way to sell the idea because you get a better sense of how this creature looks and moves. **JJ**

NEWT, TINA, QUEENIE & JACOB ENTER LOFT —

EARLY FRAMES THAT STORYBOARD THE OCCAMY SEQUENCE (1) The Demiguise leads Newt and the gang upstairs to the loft space in the department store. (2) The Demiguise enters the loft space. (3) It moves away from camera into the foreboding loft space. (4) The shot continues – as the Demiguise moves away, heads bob up into shot in the foreground. (5) Reverse angle: As the Demiguise moves past camera and out of shot the camera pushes in to reveal Newt, Tina, Queenie and Jacob at the loft entrance. (6) The shot continues – we push in to see their reaction. (7) In the same shot we see Newt and Tina enter shot and walk slowly and quietly toward the Demiguise. (8) Reverse angle past the Demiguise as we see Newt and the others getting closer.

We can see the contents of the Demiguise's handbag as it is emptied in the foreground of shot. (9) Angle on Newt as he steps into a pool of light. (10) Angle on Tina, Queenie and Jacob as they look about at their surroundings. (11) High angle as Newt steps into the light. Camera drifts down and we discover that it is in fact a P.O.V. from the Occamy. (12) The shot continues as the camera drops down on to Newt and the Demiguise. (13) P.O.V. up into the dark loft space. (14–15) The Occamy emerges out of the darkness. (16) Angle on shocked faces of Tina, Queenie and Jacob. (17) Occamy descends to face Newt and Demiguise. (18) Camera tracks round to show a tender moment between Demiguise and Occamy! **JC**

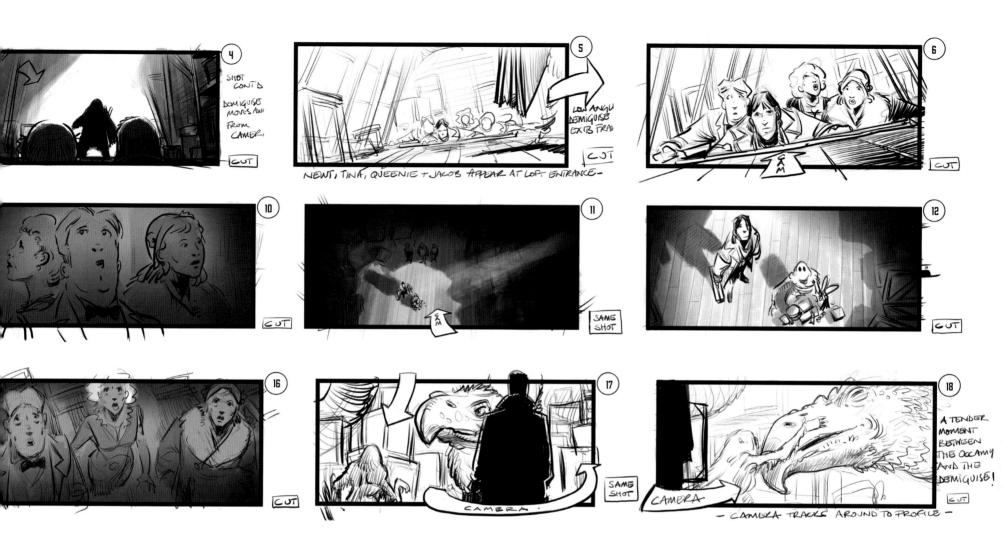

CHARACTER SKETCHES If I start storyboarding a project before it has been cast I always do character sketches. This is a shorthand that gives me a point of reference, especially at the beginning, and helps me to keep continuity amongst the characters. I usually do a single pass at this as I believe that if your brain comes up with it first it should be able to remember it. I was quite pleased with the Tina and Graves sketches (*third & seventh from left*). **GA**

↑ **THE OCCAMY** This version has slightly wilder plumage, definitely more bird than serpent. I was trying to convey the roiling movement I had in my head, a kind of ceaseless coiling. **ABRO**

↑ **THE OCCAMY** A different scale, and rather more serpent and less bird than before. **ABRO**

↑ **EARLY OCCAMY DESIGN IN DIAGRAM FORM / RB**

↑ **A FIRST ATTEMPT AT THE OCCAMY** I think this was a really difficult challenge, a winged and feathered serpent, but it had the right feeling: proud, haughty and exotic. **ABRO**

⬆ THE OCCAMY This was a collaborative work. Using concept art supplied by Boswell Production, and reference gathered by supervisors Tim Burke and Ferran Domenech, I painted over a render generated at MPC. **SM**

↑ THE OCCAMY This was a hard creature to get right, She had to look elegant and mysterious, but also needed to show a strong maternal side when threatened. To show her in a threatened state we wanted the Occamy's feathers to have an animated iridescent quality, so for inspiration we looked to birds such as the peacock for their feathers. We also looked at cuttlefish and chameleons for their changing skin patterns. **MM**

← OCCAMY HEAD STUDY For this I used, as reference, reptiles and the head crest of the secretary bird. **DB**

THE FIRST COLOUR STUDY OF THE OCCAMY After the initial round of sketches, I was looking at some tropical birds but also the humble kingfisher. **DB**

→ SKETCH OF THE THUNDERBIRD ENVIRONMENT I did this to collect my thoughts on this environment. Definitely not one for an art book but I'm including it because it shows where a lot of the more elaborate images start. Concept design at its purest! **DP**

↓ IDEA FOR THE THUNDERBIRD Here we used the multi-wing idea with the more regal look of an eagle and much less serpentine. **DB**

↑ **3D DIGITAL SKETCH OF THE THUNDERBIRD** Working in 3D really helped me work out the placement of the wings. **SR**

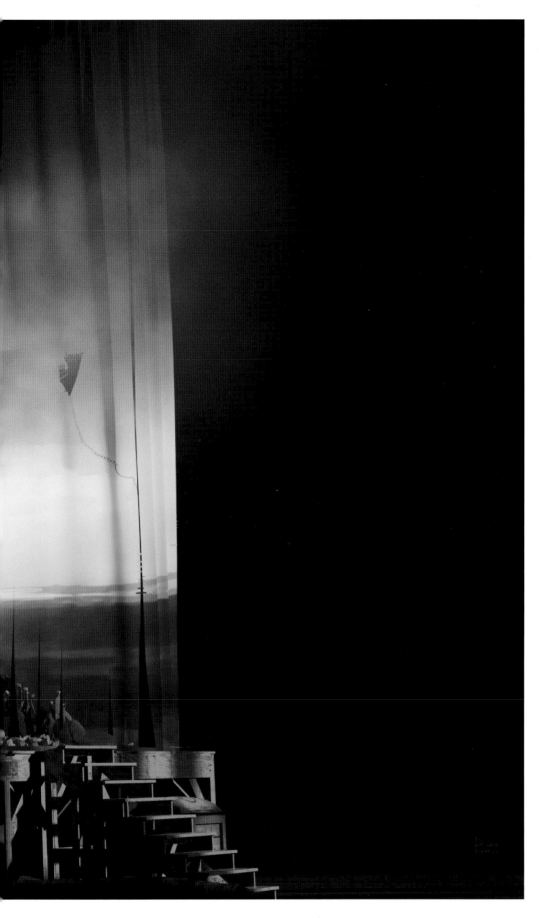

THE WILD WEST ENVIRONMENT This image (and the animation that went with it) summed up the design philosophy that we developed with Stuart for Newt's case.

Following feedback about an earlier design that it was 'too epic', I was wondering how to put these often giant and magisterial creatures in environments that are cramped and modest. Rob Bliss nailed it by pointing out that if Newt is not so preoccupied with the level of sophistication of the habitats then use that fact and make *that* be what the design is about. Once we realized that Newt is more concerned with keeping the beasts happy than demonstrating his wizarding power then we could think about what is the *least* he could do to provide a happy home for them so he could get on with what he really wants to do: take care of the creatures.

We also considered what would be around at that time to inspire him. We looked at nineteenth-century Wild West shows with beautifully painted backdrops that were often carelessly hung. Also fairground shows of the period that were very rudimentary – rough-hewn boards nailed together. The extra magic was that the 'painted' backing was animated (referencing the well-established 'living paintings' that we see in the Harry Potter stories). With this animation playing out over a backing that is torn and weathered, the artifice is obvious to the audience. (If it was too 'clean' then it would read as a landscape, not a painting of a landscape.)

The idea was that the creature inside its environment perceives the world receding to the distant horizon, it believes it is 'home' (but might suspect it is not) – not ideal, but good enough to keep them comfortable while in Newt's care. **DP**

← **THE THUNDERBIRD** In this version I am trying to resolve how those four pairs of wings could all fold together against the body. Also, adding textures from real birds on top of a ZBrush model would convey a more believable creature: lighting conditions are always important. **AV**

↑ THUNDERBIRD SKETCHES / DB

↑ **THE THUNDERBIRD** This is a painting of the Thunderbird I did which is moving away from the golden eagle colour scheme and toward a more graphic black and white. **SR**

THE THUNDERBIRD Depending on the situation and environment, the Thunderbird revealed emotion through changes in surface detail. I explored these various states by composing detailed head studies of the Thunderbird. The primary look of the character was a base of white with subtle hints of gold running through the racines of the feathers, expanding into the cells of the interlocking barbules. **KT**

THE THUNDERBIRD This creature had to feel majestic and iconic to make it stand out from existing large birds we're used to seeing. Adding extra wings was of course something that distinguished its silhouette, but we wanted to add something else to make it more fantastical.

The idea was in the name of the creature. This image depicts its thunderous state, reflecting stormy clouds, darkening the feathers as it releases its energy. **MM**

THE THUNDERBIRD IN FLIGHT This concept was created to show the full effect of the Thunderbird in flight, as it flies through the sky it generates a ferocious thunderstorm from its large wings. **DB**

↑ **THE THUNDERBIRD PRODUCING A STORM** As a magical creature, the Thunderbird is supposed to produce storms out of those four pairs of wings. This image is the idea that lightning could come out of the tips of the wings and give birth to a storm. **AV**

↓ **THE THUNDERBIRD IN FLIGHT** This series of different flying mode views from the same ZBrush model shows how the four pairs of wings could potentially open up. Here the tail was similar to birds of paradise, really delicate. This is why I love ZBrush: you can deliver so many different views in order to sell an idea. **AV**

THE THUNDERBIRD CLOSE UP Looking at adding detail variation to the structure of the individual feathers, as well as the groom around the eye and brow of the Thunderbird, I worked up orthographic studies for the 3D and CFX teams to reference. The idea of a 'bracken' feather was introduced to add another layer of detail sitting below the main groom, partially revealed through a traditional feather layout. **TR**

THE THUNDERBIRD The purpose of this image was to illustrate the nobility of the character, even in a restful pose. I painted over a base mesh render from Laurence Priest, adding an overall groom of neutral feathers and hints of colour around the beak and eye area. **KT**

THE THUNDERBIRD IN FLIGHT The same as the previous ZBrush sculpt, but the tail is thicker here with longer feathers that could fit more to a bird with that type of body shape and character. **AV**

6 AMONGST THE VARIOUS FANTASTIC BEASTS WITHIN NEWT'S CASE IS THE MAJESTIC THUNDERBIRD. I EXPLORED THE IDEA OF AN ORNATE CELL STRUCTURE WITHIN THE FEATHERS OF THE THUNDERBIRD, VISIBLE WHEN THE CHARACTER WAS BACK-LIT. I REFERENCED THE ETHEREAL QUALITIES OF VARIOUS STAINED-GLASS STRUCTURES, SUCH AS THE ABSTRACT DESIGN WORK OF THE ARTIST JOHN PIPER. 9

THE THUNDERBIRD / KT

5

THE BLIND PIG

THE BLIND PIG The famous New York Speakeasy! In our world we have The Blind Pig, a version of the Leaky Cauldron, populated with wizards, witches and all kinds of magical creatures and lorded over by the goblin, Gnarlak. **PPOP**

↑ **THE BAR ELF** For this character I used photographic reference for the skin textures to give it some realism. For this reason, I kept the eyes small rather than the usual larger elf eyes. **PC**

➡ **THE CLIENTELE AT THE BLIND PIG** This was completed after brainstorming ideas of who might frequent The Blind Pig. After a few too many cocktails, some cantankerous wizards have a bar fight and after they make up they are left with the result of their slurred spells. **PC**

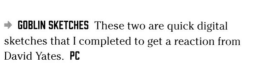

→ GOBLIN SKETCHES These two are quick digital sketches that I completed to get a reaction from David Yates. PC

THE BLIND PIG BAR SCENE I really enjoyed doing the series of black and white sketches of bar scenes (*this page, and opposite*). Most creature designs have a single creature on a page, where these hopefully show a bit of personality in their interaction. The lack of colour also helps place them in the period of the film. **PC**

⬆ **MUG SHOT OF A NEW YORK GOBLIN** More of a street urchin type. **RB**

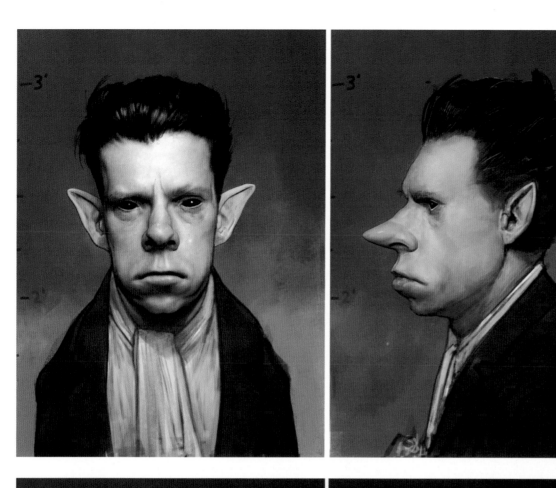

ANOTHER MUG SHOT This was a great way of showing off goblin designs and placing them in the twenties. **RB**

NEW YORK GOBLIN GENT Another chance to mix dapper and disturbing. **RB**

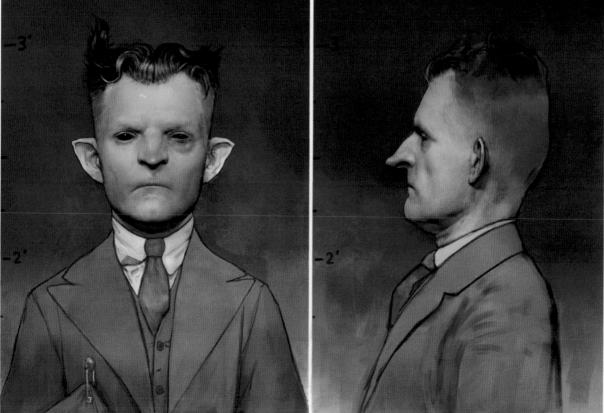

THE CLIENTELE AT THE BLIND PIG A particularly favourable aspect of working in 3D is being able to produce multiple angles of a given scenario. **RB**

◄◄ THE BLIND PIG CLIENTELE SHEET These head sheets were put together to show prospective looks for the various 'types' frequenting The Blind Pig, including: a tattooed lady; three witchy sisters; female goblins; the spirit of a native American; and a gangster ghost sporting his bullet holes. **RB**

⬇ NEW YORK GOBLIN WITH FANCY HAT Prospective goblin for The Blind Pig. Notice he has two thousand fingers. **RB**

⬆ NEW YORK GOBLIN / RB

⬆ GOBLIN WAITER I liked the idea of a goblin being servile and very polite yet utterly disconcerting to look at. **RB**

⬅ A GOBLIN The time and setting of the story provided the opportunity to design a few goblins sporting a relatively modern look, to show how goblins might dress up for a decent night of illegal drinking, impressing the ladies and fist fighting. One sports a fancy hat, all have more than their fair share of fingers. **RB**

⬆ A GOBLIN GENTLEMAN WHO HAPPENS TO BE DATING A FLAPPER / RB

↞ **EARLY DESIGNS FOR GOBLIN JAZZ BAND THAT PLAYS IN THE BLIND PIG SPEAKEASY** From left to right: very early sketch of a goblin musician, the banjo survived to end up stuck on the side of the double bass; goblin close-up, a one-man brass section; the piano player, whose goblin hands allow him to play more than an octave with each one; early design of goblin buddies, I think the character on the left ended up being used for the drummer. **RB**

↑ **GNARLAK DESIGN** At some point we gave goblins seven fingers per hand, possibly a consequence from needing more fingers to play instruments in the jazz band. **RB**

THE JAZZ SINGER IN THE BLIND PIG This was the first sketch of the prospective singer with The Blind Pig jazz band. I recall she was out of the band for a while but I left this picture pinned on the wall behind me. And, as chance would have it, it eventually found favour again. **RB**

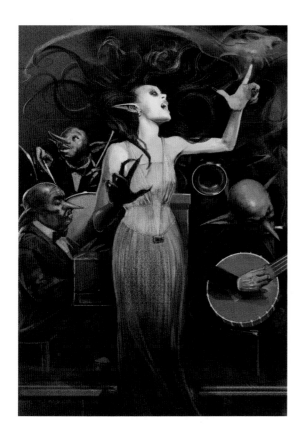

GOBLIN BAND AND SINGER This was an attempt at illustrating the goblin band as a 1920s jazz band with a Siren-like singer whose hair floated mesmerizingly in slow motion around her as if underwater. **PC**

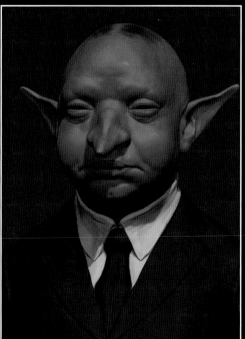

← **THE JAZZ SINGER IN THE BLIND PIG** Dermot and I had many conversations about the lighting, for this concept, and it was probably worth it. **RB**

← **PORTRAITS OF THE GOBLIN JAZZ BAND** These portraits of the goblins that play in The Blind Pig's jazz band were done as facial reference for the visual effects department. In the portrait of the drummer (*top*) I was trying to make him less like a goblin, while still separating him from your average homo sapien. Pointed ears obviously help with the process. The middle portrait is of the pianist, and the bottom one is of the 'one-man' brass section. I originally drew him blowing into one of his many instruments, but then drew him in this neutral pose to aid the VFX department. **RB**

↑ **THE BLIND PIG JAZZ BAND** The band originally consisted of four male goblins. The goblin playing the double bass was removed after the (re-) arrival of the lady goblin on vocals. **RB**

← **THE BLIND PIG JAZZ BAND** Sometimes limitation can be a useful aspect of design. We had a lot of instruments needing to be played but only four goblins to play them all so, out of practical necessity, the overworked goblin acting as the brass section became a multi-instrumentalist. When we added a singer the quartet of players became a trio. **RB**

⬆ CHARACTER STUDIES OF THE JAZZ SINGER IN THE BLIND PIG / RB

➡➡ THE FULL LINE-UP OF THE GOBLIN SPEAKEASY BAND FRONTED BY THEIR FEMALE VOCALIST The period microphone wasn't strictly necessary but it was a nice visual addition. RB

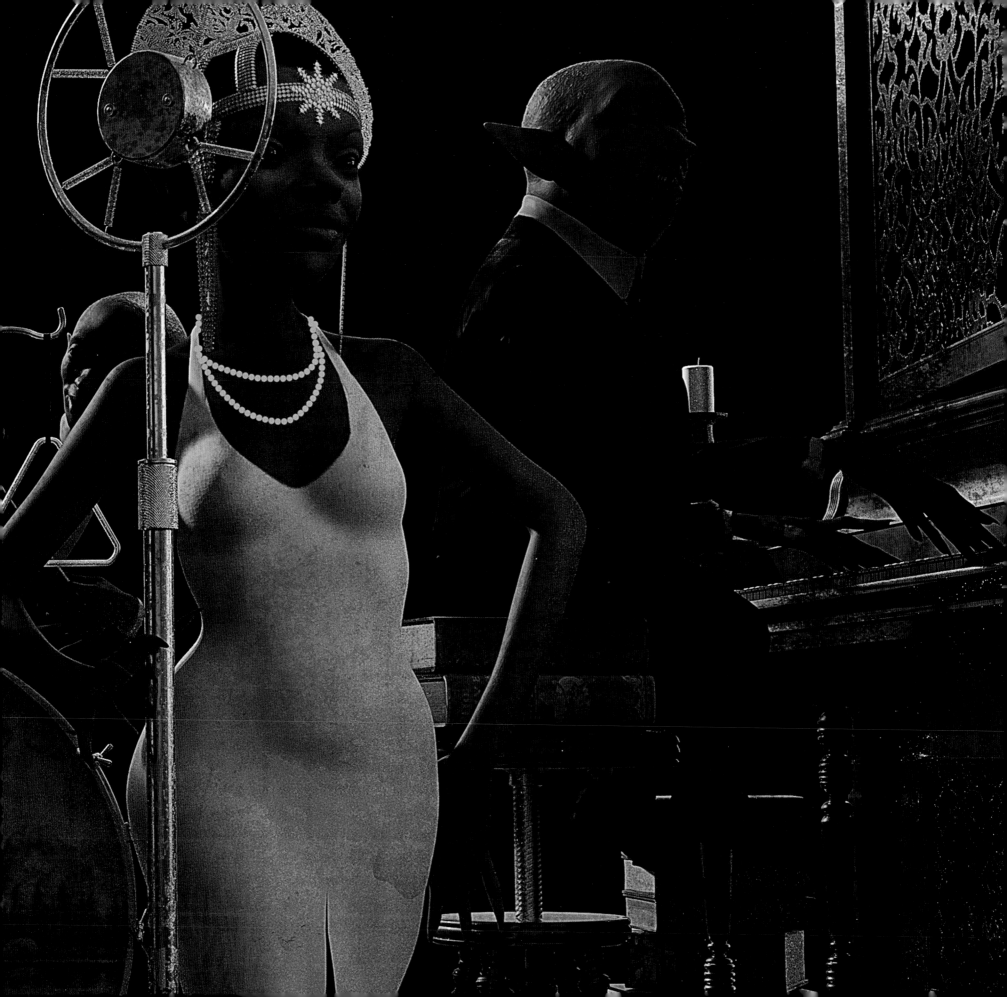

THE JAZZ SINGER IN THE BLIND PIG Whilst referencing earlier concept work from Rob Bliss and Pablo Grillo we gave her goblin proportions whilst retaining her femininity, as well as ageing her a little to be more like Billie Holiday or Ella Fitzgerald in their prime. With references from our hair and makeup designer Fae Hammond, we designed a makeup that helped accent her black eyes – making them as alluring as possible. Her features were a key reference point in creating an attractive, sensual character as briefed by David Yates. **VH, KS, SM, MB, DH, DS**

JAZZ-PIPES Stuart Craig came up with the idea that the goblin brass player might have a set of bagpipes. It sounded crazy, but my design actually looked really effective and proved that Stuart is always right even when it seems like he might be wrong. **RB**

⬆ **GNARLAK DESIGN** I distorted photographic references of aged skin to help achieve a higher level of realism to Gnarlak's craggy, weathered face in this early series of concepts. I also tried invoking 1950s screen actors like Spencer Tracy and Kirk Douglas. **PC**

➡ **GNARLAK DESIGN** These two were completed after knowing that actor Ron Perlman would be playing Gnarlak. We were trying very hard to keep Ron's distinctive look but I found that, by adding traditionally goblin features like a long nose, his distinctive looks started to disappear and become someone entirely different. **PC**

6
THE OBSCURUS

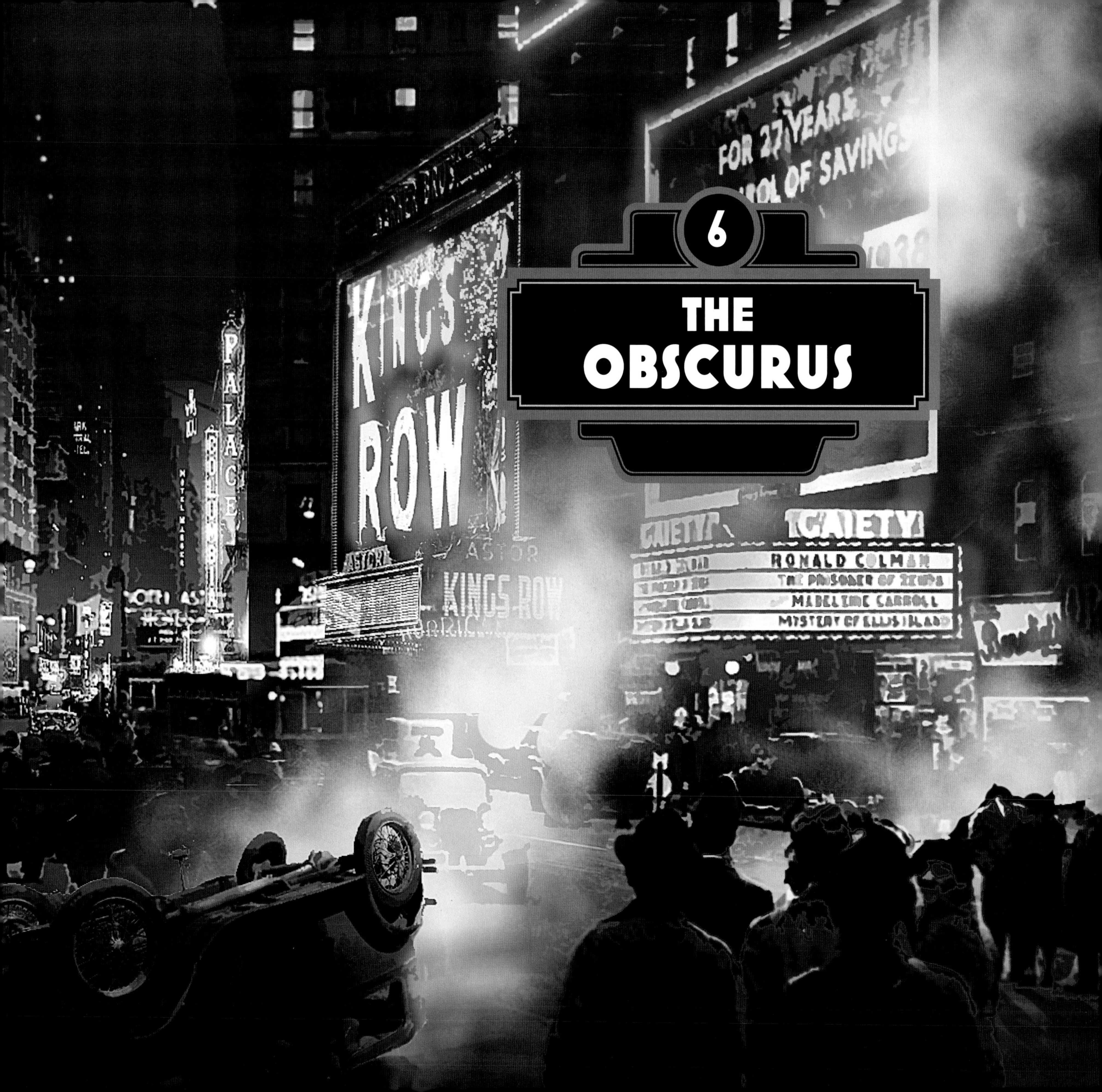

I started working on the Obscurus during the first two weeks of work on the project. I loved the challenge of capturing such a unique entity and worked hard to portray the look of an invisible being in a cloud of dust. **MK**

◄◄ **TIMES SQUARE** The hustle and bustle of old New York feels almost contemporary, despite it being a time before neon had even been invented. Like most of my work for *Fantastic Beasts* this illustration (and the one on pp. 248–9) is a result of a group effort. My time on the project had almost run out and I was already committed to a new job when Stuart asked me to come up with concepts for the Times Square set on a Friday afternoon. I remember sketching it out on a weekend after Hayley had set up buildings in 3D and the set decoration team provided plan views and research. **PPOP**

➡ **THE OBSCURUS** I was asked to show the Obscurus trapped in a box or tablet shape. I like the idea of who very different ideas colliding, the rigid square box and the swirling almost liquid force that yearns to be released. **DB**

⬆ **BROKEN CHANDELIER** I built this chandelier in 3D and conceptualized it for Stuart and the art director in charge of the location in Liverpool. The props art director wanted to show the level of destruction attained as it fell from the roof while still attached by its power cord. **TW**

⬆ **TORN SHAW CAMPAIGN BANNER** The 'hero' scenic painting was huge, detailed and beautiful. The visual was done after the canvas was finished as a means to explore the extent to which the Obscurus wrecks it along with the political stage. We only had one chance to tear the portrait to match Stuart's desired look so he sketched an outline for where to make the rips and gave me a description of the marks it was to have left. A scaled version of the visual was then used as a guide by the prop department for where and how to make the damage. For the approval process, they did test pieces showing smoke marks, and various ripped and burnt edges. The look was intended to convey the entity's huge force and sinister nature, without defining its mode of destruction. Left precariously suspended, the torn and smouldering image of Shaw is identifiable but greatly diminished to create a lingering sense of threat. **MS**

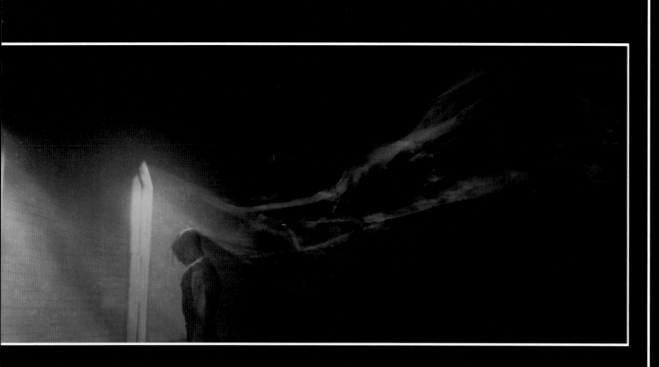

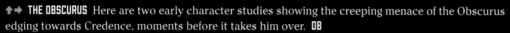

↑→ THE OBSCURUS Here are two early character studies showing the creeping menace of the Obscurus edging towards Credence, moments before it takes him over. **DB**

↓ CREDENCE AND THE OBSCURUS Another Credence and Obscurus study showing the Obscurus as something barely tangible, visibly, yet oozing power and malevolence. **DB**

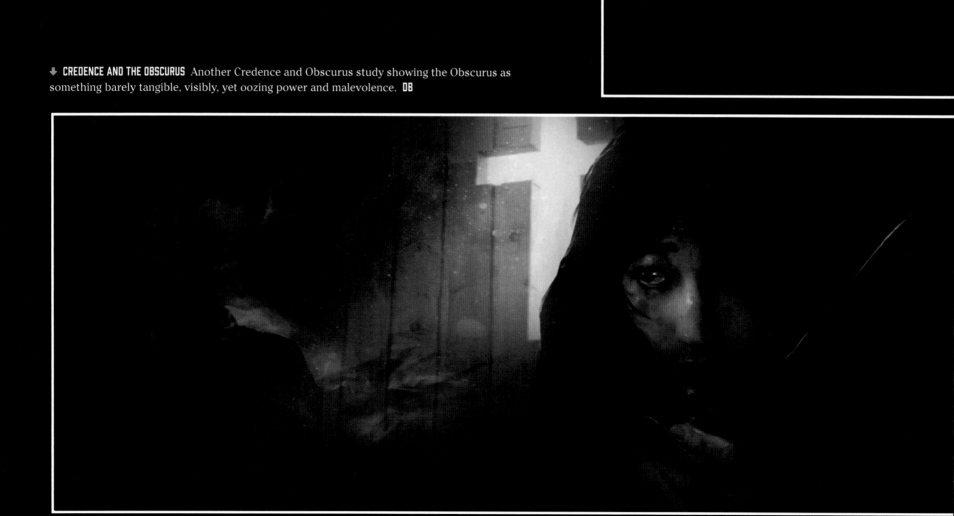

⬆ **EARLY IDEA FOR THE OBSCURUS IN A SUITCASE** The parameters had already been set by David and J.K. Rowling about it being in a glass enclosure, like a vial the size of a carrier bag, which made me immediately think of Damien Hirst. **GM**

⬅ **THE OBSCURUS** A further study showing the box idea, this time made from a more organic mass, with a hint of what is kept inside. **DB**

THE OBSCURUS In this variation of the Obscurus, a young girl suffering from her repressed magic is bound by a rectangular shell. I created this image to illustrate the anguish of this tormented soul. **KT**

THE OBSCURUS This set of concepts was composed to illustrate the progression of Credence transforming into the Obscurus. The Obscurus material consumes Credence until human shapes are difficult to discern. The challenge was pushing the design towards something unique and unfamiliar. **KT**

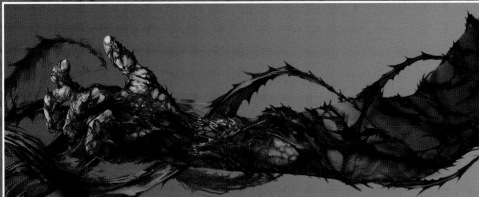

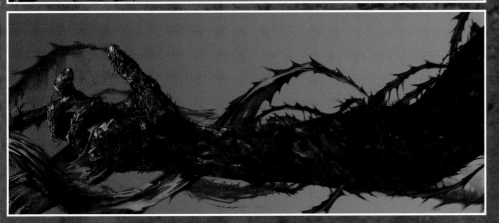

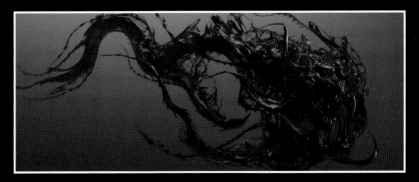

⬆ **438 AN EARLY TEST OF THE OBSCURUS** Referencing the artwork of Russ Mills, this exercise was an attempt to embed features of Credence in an abstract manner using a base sculpt of Ezra Miller by Kouji Tajima. Early ideas of surface movement included extracting sound data from performances of Ezra Miller and using the information to drive effects simulations in Houdini. **FV**

⬆ **AN EARLY ZBRUSH CONCEPT OF THE OBSCURUS MONSTER FACE** At this stage, we were exploring subtleties of colour on the surface of the Obscurus material to introduce another narrative device for conveying emotion. To move away from the overall shape of the Obscurus looking like an 'angry ball', we worked on abstracting the core form, referencing sculptors Umberto Boccioni and Barbara Hepworth. **KT**

➡ **EVOLUTION OF THE OBSCURUS FACE** In these studies I attempted to illustrate the evolution of the Obscurus face. I extracted elements of 'Obscurus membrane' from a 3D render by Frederic Valleur and, while referencing images of Ezra Miller, distorted the material into recognizable features of Credence. **TR**

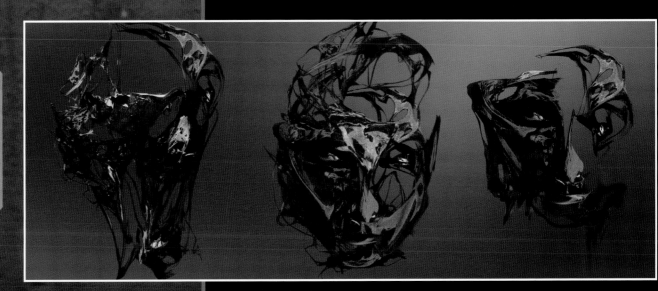

⬇ **THE OBSCURUS** The Obscurus is all swirling dark matter, similar to oil. **MK**

⬆ **FIRST SKETCH FOR THE OBSCURUS** The idea was it would always be moving between either a gas, liquid or a solid state. I wanted most areas to be vague with hints of a face or a limb moving in and out of the obscurity. **SR**

⬇ **THE OBSCURUS** This is a sketch sequence done on my first day on the project. Here, I tried to imagine the unseen character of the Obscurus in my sketches. **MK**

→ THE OBSCURUS CAUSING DESTRUCTION The Obscurus was one of the most challenging visual tasks I encountered. In this image I was asked to show it smashing through the windows of a New York building and gliding down the facade. The idea here was to visualize the Obscurus through the use of the falling debris which, touching his invisible body, would show the audience quick glimpses of his outline and shapes. The final effect was achieved through a subtle manipulation of the particle cloud, revealing the Obscurus' outline in just a few places and just enough to show the audience that something mysterious is moving in the debris. **FC**

↑ THE OBSCURUS' FACE Early on in the development of the Obscurus, we began referencing artwork by various artists, such as Russ Mills, to explore the idea of emotion through bold lines and abstract shapes. I produced various portraits of the actor using traditional media, such as charcoal, acrylic and oil on paper. **TR**

→→ TIMES SQUARE. / PPOP

" THE DEVELOPMENT OF NEW YORK CITY IS VERY WELL DOCUMENTED IN CONTEMPORARY PHOTOGRAPHY. BUT IN ORDER TO TELL OUR STORY WE NEEDED TO FIND ANGLES THAT HADN'T BEEN SEEN BEFORE. AFTER I PROJECTED AN OLD PHOTOGRAPH ON A 3D GEOMETRY OF THE CITY WE WERE ABLE TO CHANGE THE PERSPECTIVE TO EXACTLY THE ANGLE WE WANTED. "

NEW YORK, AS SEEN FROM ABOVE / PPOP

THE OBSCURUS' DESTRUCTION This image illustrates several set pieces from different places that would be built partly on our backlot and partly on location in Liverpool. It was my task to create a believable environment, using digital set extensions for the background areas. **PPOP**

THE OBSCURUS' DESTRUCTION The reverse of the view on the previous pages showing more damage done to the subway station beneath. **PPOP**

➡ **FOUR STORYBOARDS SHOWING TINA, NEWT, QUEENIE AND JACOB** A reverse angle shows Newt, Tina and Jacob looking out over New York from the rooftop vantage point; tighter shot as the group of friends look out over New York from the rooftop; the view from the rooftop past our heroes as we see the trail of destruction across New York; Newt, Tina, Queenie and Jacob Disapparate on to a rooftop in an attempt to track the Obscurus. **JC**

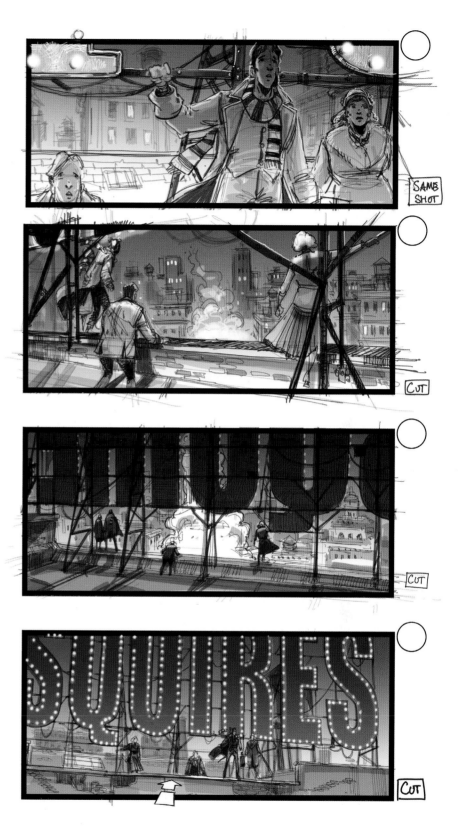

➡➡ **THE OBSCURUS' DESTRUCTION** Sometimes sets are built only to be torn down again. This illustration was investigating the amount of damage done to the subway station during the final showdown. **PPOP**

THE OBSCURUS STORYBOARD SEQUENCE These were difficult to draw because there were few firm ideas about the Obscurus' appearance and its abilities. This led to a series of key frame studies based around Credence and the Obscurus' possession of his body.

How would the Obscurus enter and exit his host and what would it/he look like?

Are they always attached in some way or are there moments of separation? Fun ideas that make Credence look a little like a rag doll or puppet on a string. (1) Credence being consumed by the Obscurus. (2) The Obscurus as a wave of pure evil drags Credence like a rag doll behind it. (3) Credence under the control of the Obscurus. (4) Credence is consumed by the black mass of the Obscurus. (5) Credence within the Obscurus. (6) The Obscurus as a shadow that follows Credence. (7) The Obscurus leaves Credence's body. (8) The Obscurus protects Credence as he rests. (9) Credence, the host for the Obscurus. (10) The Obscurus enters Credence. (11) The Obscurus and Credence are one. Frames 2, 4, 6 & 8 are more elaborate and finished frames – drawn in an attempt to sell certain concepts and ideas whilst developing the final act. 1920s New York streets proved a fun setting for the finale of the film. **JC**

THE OBSCURUS At the earliest stages of the work, I had very little information about the Obscurus, so I just experimented with different materials. **MK**

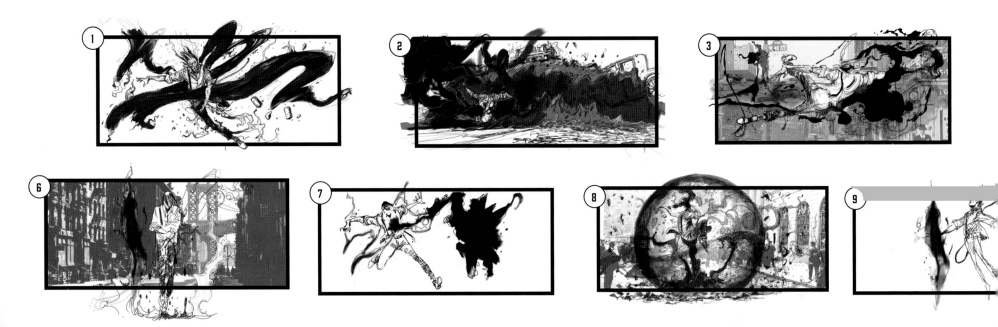

⬆ **THE OBSCURUS** Here it rises from a cloud of smoke and dust. **MK**

⬆ **THE OBSCURUS** Shown here as an abstract mass of glowing matter. **MK**

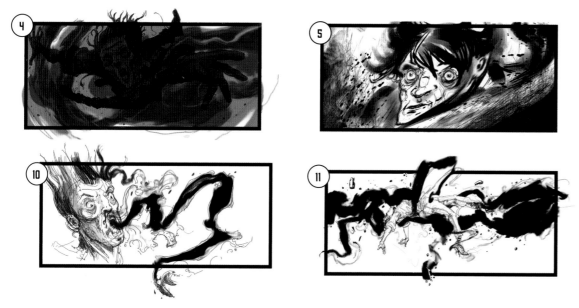

⬇ **EARLY MOTION STUDY OF THE OBSCURUS** This series of four images show how once the Obscurus is let loose, and possibly invisible, we would get glimpses of its form through distortion of its surroundings. In this case turning a car in to an orange peel-like sculpture, a swirling mass of broken glass and metal, blasting its way through the streets of New York. **DB**

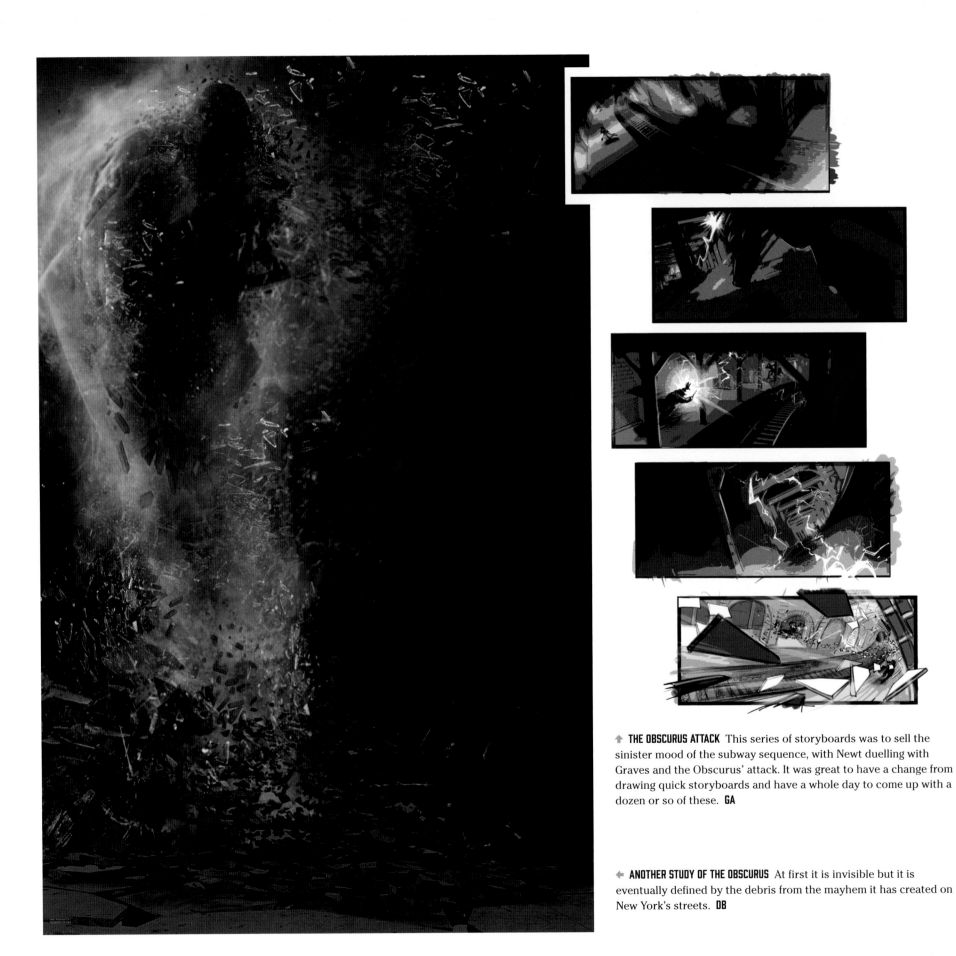

↑ THE OBSCURUS ATTACK This series of storyboards was to sell the sinister mood of the subway sequence, with Newt duelling with Graves and the Obscurus' attack. It was great to have a change from drawing quick storyboards and have a whole day to come up with a dozen or so of these. **GA**

← ANOTHER STUDY OF THE OBSCURUS At first it is invisible but it is eventually defined by the debris from the mayhem it has created on New York's streets. **DB**

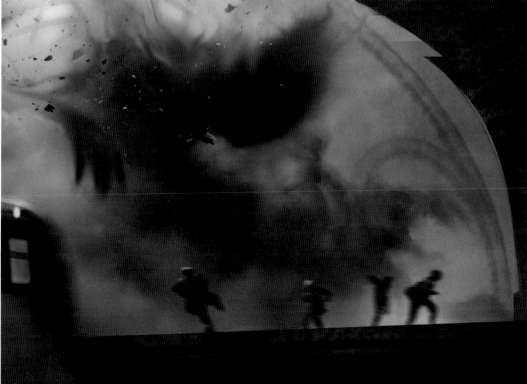

↑ **VERY EARLY IDEA FOR THE OBSCURUS** The idea here is that the afflicted person would expel a sort of ectoplasm mass that would engulf the person, eventually growing and taking control with the person trapped inside. **DB**

← **THE OBSCURUS ATTACK** The Obscurus is the most complex character: just imagine that you need to draw an invisible villain. During the first few days of work I was in a state of shock! **MK**

THE OBSCURUS This series was an attempt to explore the Obscurus in motion, a chaotic mass of energy. The challenge was to create something with enough weight and structure to believably wreak havoc and cause destruction to the surrounding environment. Our solution was to reference sculptures of artists, such as Barbara Hepworth and Henry Moore, to create a core form for the Obscurus that would transform over the duration of a shot. As an appendage of the Obscurus bears weight, its mass evolves. The core form was animated, then handed over to the effects team to produce a simulation that would give surface detail and character to the overall look of the Obscurus. **KT, FV, PP**

THE OBSCURUS' MONSTER FACE For very brief moments, we see the suggestion of the warped 'monster face' of the Obscurus. This face embodies the distorted anguish and evil torment of Credence's suppressed magic. I worked up a sculpt in ZBrush which was then refined by Thomas Bolt. **KT, FV**

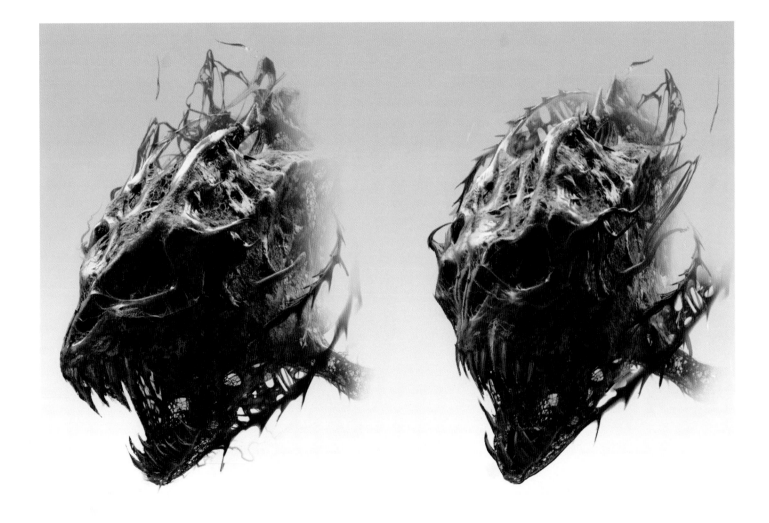

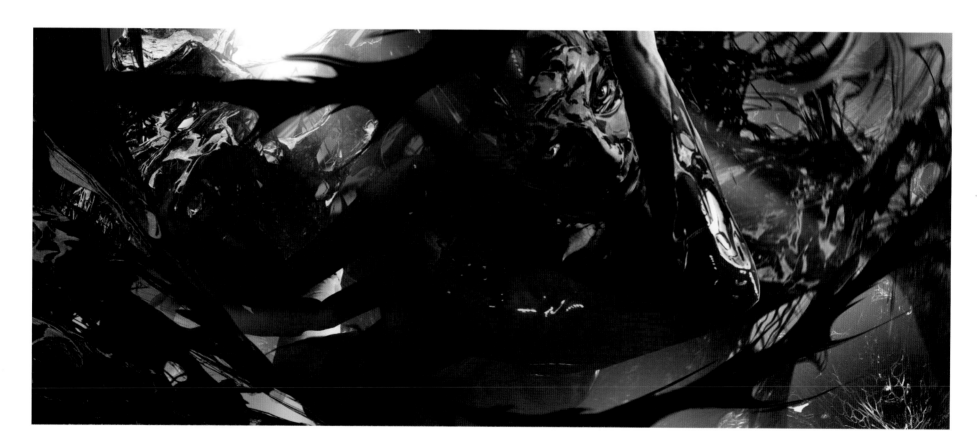

⬆ **CREDENCE AND THE OBSCURUS' MONSTER FACE** Credence is constrained within the core of the Obscurus, a tangled nest of membranes and tendrils. Using a distorted base model of Ezra Miller by David Frylund Otzen, Tania Richard composed this image to explore the bound abstraction of Credence whilst retaining recognizable features such as the character's eyes. **TR, DFO**

➡➡ **THE OBSCURUS** The purpose of this concept was to explore motion, destruction and the evolution of form within a shot as the Obscurus blindly smashes through the streets of New York. We went through various incarnations of the Obscurus, inspired by the emotional performances of Ezra Miller, from abstract and distorted shapes to a classic creature design. Kouji Tajima attempted to convey in this image a sense of the creature within a chaotic mass of membranes and lashing appendages. **KT**

AERIAL SHOT OF NEW YORK I painted this image as one of a series of aerial shots to show the shape of New York at the time of the story. It was a challenge to show the scale and complexity of the structures whilst keeping the mood and atmosphere. **TW**